The VERY ORDINARY STORY of a VERY ORDINARY FAMILY

Peggy Boult

With love
Peggy.

Margaretta 'Peggy' Dorothy Marshall Boult

The
VERY ORDINARY STORY
of a
VERY ORDINARY FAMILY

Peggy Boult

Published by Duncan Brown
Produced by RKM Communications, London

All rights reserved; no part of this publication may be reproduced or transmitted by any means, electronic, mechanical, photocopying or otherwise, without the prior permission of the publisher.

While the publishers have made reasonable effort to trace the copyright owners for any or all of the photographs in this book, there may be some omissions of credits for which we apologise.

First published in Great Britain in 2005 by
Duncan Brown, 190 Kings Hall Road, Beckenham, Kent BR3 1LJ

Copyright © Margaretta Boult 2005

The moral rights of the author have been asserted.

ISBN 0-9549697-0-7

Printed and bound in United Kingdom of Great Britain.
by Fraser Hamilton Associates Ltd

*To amuse the grandchildren
in later years...*

~ Foreword ~

My grandmother was born on 18th April 1915 in Salisbury, Rhodesia and died on 11th August 1996 in Scarborough hospital after suffering a heart attack. She was an intensely private person and although very close to those she loved she still kept so much to herself. Her diaries reveal much of her wonderful life and experiences and such a record has enormous value for our family and ensures that her memories survive for future generations.

She was of course like any other grandmother; kind and generous especially with her afternoon teas where you'd be lucky to escape with only double helpings, such was her desire for you to grow up big and strong. Best of all was when you arrived at her house unannounced looking for a cup of tea or a beer, where you could be assured that you would be received with a very warm welcome, no matter the circumstance.

She was a witty and intelligent lady, though happy playing second fiddle to Grandpa Ben's more extrovert personality. She must have listened to his jokes and stories on countless occasions but each time was as if it was her first, delighting in the fun of it all; a role she was happy to fulfil, such was the strength of their relationship. She was known to have suffered greatly from agoraphobia, though as grandchildren we did not seem to notice. She was a staunch supporter of the Monarchy which was mirrored by her love of corgis and never missing the Queen's speech on Christmas Day!

Her memoirs cover the years either side of WW2 and are so vastly different to the years of early 2000. She never complained about their situation, no matter how dire, preferring to focus on the adventures that would be lying ahead. There is no indication of bitterness towards the harsh realities of war: the injuries and deaths of friends and colleagues; and not knowing whether she had said goodbye to Ben for the last time prior to his many 'sorties'. These features, together with other tragic events, were all part of wartime life and like everybody else, she just had to accept them.

Her story naturally focuses around her husband who was an extraordinary man: a gifted pilot, commanding exceptional respect from those in the Royal Air Force; a wonderful husband; a caring father and a fun-loving grandfather. It becomes clear that throughout their lives they had little material concerns; money, or the lack of it, never seemed to feature highly as there were greater things to worry about – how different life was back then!

Should my grandparents ever have had a motto I am sure it would have been something like 'enjoy life' and this is why this story is such a great read. This book is an important insight into everyday life during a period of major social, economic and political transition and remains pertinent to all future generations.

Publishing her 'story' is my tribute to them both and an illustration of how to live life to the full. Finally, and I suppose most importantly, it is an exceptional love story and an inspiration to us all.

The Grandchildren – DRLB
1 January 2005

~ Chapter One ~

I WAS BORN IN AFRICA

I was brought up by Comfort, not *in* comfort! – for Comfort was the name of our homely, huge and ever patient African nanny. I can see her now appearing each morning in the bright blue and white uniform supplied by my mother, her head swathed in a faded Union Jack unwittingly supplied by His Majesty. She was of vast proportions and we led her an awful life, but I can never recall her being the least bit angry. I always picture her shaking her head with a large grin from ear to ear and saying, "No, no Miss Peggy, no do dat," but joining in the fun all the same. She had a large family of her own, about eleven children I think. African mothers seem to be gifted with a supreme calmness somehow and it takes a lot to ruffle them, and I suppose my brother's and my antics were nothing much to worry about. She was also a bit of a prophetess and I distinctly recall her telling my mother one morning in pidgin English that I was going to, "Walk-a-walk too far," for my two front teeth had a large gap between them! She proved to be correct, although at that time none of us could have foreseen the future events that were to take place. The years have been full of great happiness and even sadness, but it has all been so worthwhile and I wouldn't have changed a single thing.

I was born in 1915 in Salisbury, Rhodesia, then an almost unheard of and very new country. My father had tossed a coin to decide whether he should go there or China, and Rhodesia won. To that coin I shall always be full of gratitude, for my young days were exciting and my country perhaps the most perfect on God's earth – I think so anyway! Daddy had gone out to join the Customs and Excise and had walked alongside an ox wagon from Mafeking to Bulawayo taking, I believe, about a fortnight or three weeks. When he was sent to Beira, in Portuguese East Africa, he sent for my mother to come too and join him so that they could be married. My mother duly arrived in the early days of 1914, complete with flannel trousseau! This of course was completely useless in the hot, humid heat and she was very miserable for many months.

Eventually my father was posted to Salisbury, where I made my appearance, and then was moved to Umtali where my brother Marshall was born. My earliest remembrance of those days is seeing my fond father climb onto the roof of the veranda, with a carving knife in hand, after a large snake which disappeared into the rain guttering. I do not know whether or not he killed the snake. About this time too he was out shooting in the veldt and another party, out doing the same thing, saw the long grass move and took aim, only to shoot my father in the right eye which he subsequently lost. The eye was replaced by a glass one which caused much fear and trembling amongst the then uncivilised natives. I remember him telling us how on his trek to Bulawayo in 1896 they harnessed three zebra to the wagon when the horses died.

My father was an amazing man. He was gentle, kind and never known to swear, and yet was full of determination and bravery. My mother tells how bitterly disappointed he was not to be able to go to war because of the loss of his eye and how plucky he was about having it removed after the accident. I can actually remember him telling me that he had had all his teeth out without an injection! He had a spare glass eye which he used to leave on the table when he went away for a few days at times. The servants were petrified at the sight of it, as was I, and they were convinced that it was watching them, so never failed in their duties.

My mother was not really happy in those pioneering days, for she had been brought up in the quietness of a Devonshire vicarage and was not the sort ever to get used to roughing it and yet she too was full of pluck, for it was no mean adventure to set out on one's own in 1914. I gather she had lots of opposition from her family. She never grumbled and I can see her now, armed with a broom chasing large, hairy hunting spiders and declaring that she was the bravest woman on earth! I am inclined to agree, for they are beastly creatures and one house we had in particular, in Bulawayo on the edge of the veldt, seemed to be full of them. It was in this house that I got my first real night-time fright. My bedroom was at the end of a line of four rooms and the outside door was always on a short chain so that it could be opened a few inches to let in a breeze, but not allow anyone to gain entry. For some unknown reason I awoke in the early hours of the morning and can remember still, with shuddering horror, the sight of a large brown hand, in full moonlight, feeling its way around that chain to see if it could be removed. I lay quite still for some seconds and then screamed. My father appeared at full speed, but by that time the door had been slammed and we could hear the sound of rushing footsteps. No harm had been done, except perhaps that is why I am still unhappy about being left alone in a house all night.

I spent my schooling days in Bulawayo apart from one year in 1925 when my father was invited to go over to the Wembley Exhibition and took us all with him. I was most unhappy there and longed for the freedom of the veldt and the warmth and sunshine. We lived on the very outskirts of Bulawayo then, as I have already said, and I can so well remember sleeping on the veranda at night under a mosquito net, with the legs of the bed in cans of water to prevent the ants from crawling over one, and falling asleep listening to the stamps of a small gold mine about three miles away. I can remember, too, bringing back chunks of granite from the same mine and crushing them optimistically in the bath, but never finding anything. I don't think there was much gold anyway at that particular mine, for it closed down after a few years even though it went under the name of Bulawayo Main Reef.

So many things spring to mind: lying in bed with typhoid fever and gazing at a pair of gorgeous black patent leather shoes which had been given to me, and wondering when I would be well enough to wear them (the typhoid was a severe lesson in disobedience, for I had knowingly drunk un-boiled water in the park!); remembrance of a green mamba in the hall and shrieks for the boy to deal with it; remembrance too of a black mamba reclining in the morning glory creeper of the tennis court and my father taking aim at it while the garden boy placed a bucket of boiling water underneath it, in case it fell only wounded; and the sight of my mother returning from playing golf one morning with a huge thirteen foot python strapped on to the back of her bicycle. She had killed it in a donga, or dry river bed, while searching for a ball and brought the snake home as proof positive for my father, who otherwise might have treated the story as that of 'the one that got away'.

There were happier and prettier thoughts of: lovely picnics in the Matopos and walks up to Rhodes' Grave and the Shangani Memorial; heavenly sunsets and music (on gramophone records) out on the lawn at nights while collecting glow worms; the beautiful garden we had with its three hedges each higher than the other of blue plumbago, yellow tecoma and red poinsettias and then the blue jacaranda trees in the background; and walks across the burnt veldt with the new green shoots springing up and flowers which seemed to come from dark dry earth as if by miracle, to give the ground the look that 'God's in his heaven and all was right with the world'.

There were funny thoughts too: how when the first water borne sewerage was installed, our cookboy washed his shirt in the toilet and was most put out when it disappeared when he pulled the chain; when a terrified houseboy refused to bring in the lighted Christmas pudding, which we ate together with the turkey and all its trimmings in extreme heat and usually accompanied by a thunderstorm; the exciting smell of the hot earth after the first rain for six months; and the dreaded sight of swarm upon swarm of locusts. I can remember when the locusts were so bad one year that the train actually stopped running, for the line was so slippery with dead bodies. There were plagues of caterpillars which ate everything and anything; white ants which did the same; and then there were the thrilling two and a half yearly trips to the seaside, usually to the Cape or Natal, about a thousand miles away which meant a three day train journey.

On one occasion, which I was too young to remember, my mother set off from Umtali to the Kowie with two small bairns and a nanny and spent five days in a train marooned on the banks of the Kowie River, as the bridges had been washed away. She eventually crossed it on pontoons and continued on her way. I expect that was the reason why my mother always gave us the impression that when she travelled she took the *lot* with her such as pieces of string, candles, flasks of whisky, and tins of biscuits, or so it seemed – once bitten twice shy!

All this and much else went up to make my childhood very happy and full of variety, in spite of the fact that we never had a telephone. Most of the time we had to walk down the garden path to answer the call of nature in a little shed where there was a bucket in a hole in the ground which was emptied each dawn by the night patrol, as the sanitary boys were called. We had a horse and cart and latterly a model 'T' Ford. There were no fridges, fans or buses that we feel we cannot live without these days – and no airmail. There was no pathological laboratory; and on one occasion when I was very ill, the doctor took the usual blood sample thinking that I had malaria again. He then had to put the specimen on the train which took it to Pretoria, and then three days later a telegram would come with the result. This time the results proved that I had not got fever, but in the meantime an abscess had burst in my left ear, and of course the quinine treatment I was having was all wrong!

I suppose it seems ridiculous now to say that I can remember the first

Imperial Airways 'flying machine' that ever came to Rhodesia, but it is absolutely true, and I am not yet seventy-seven years old! I was taken to the airfield to watch this historic event, clutching in my hand a coin which my father had placed on the railway track in front of the first train that ever entered Bulawayo Station.

School I was never fond of, but realised it was a thing that had to be put up with and I actually tolerated the last year when, I am ashamed to say, I was 'someone' and my leaving days were in sight. Somehow I managed to pass the Senior Cambridge exam and then did the usual course in shorthand and typing. Although I had always wanted to be a music teacher, family funds would not rise to the training, for my brother had to have much specialist treatment for his eyes. Marshall had been born with perfect sight, but some poisonous dust had entered them and formed a kind of film. One eye was scarred and so he was never able to go to school or lead a normal life as far as playing games etc was concerned. Yet he was the most cheerful person and on occasion, when he was in hospital lying in the dark with bandages on for six weeks, he used to whistle to himself and was then christened 'The Canary'. Eventually he underwent some treatment by some Germans whereby the film, which was too thin to be removed by a surgeon's knife, was needled back, but this procedure could only be done a certain number of times. The result of this treatment was that one of his eyes is divided by a line: a blue eye in one half; and an opaque piece filling the remainder. At least it meant that he could see a little with the aid of very strong glasses and a magnifying glass.

At the end of my training I went to Salisbury to live with my father who was now separated from my mother which was a tremendous upheaval for me. It took a long time to realise that I had no proper home, for I was living in a hostel and my father in a boarding house. Inwardly I had known this was going to happen for years and I shall always be grateful to my parents for staying together while we were young. They were just completely incompatible but I loved them equally. Before I went to live in Salisbury I had spent a gorgeous holiday with a school friend there, three weeks in which we went to seventeen dances in twenty-two days! No wonder I was anxious to leave school. It was then that I met a very nice boy whom I got very fond of and nearly married! He told me that his first impression of me was that I had, "nice eyes, but rather funny legs"!

Eventually I became qualified and got a job with the Medical Department. Apparently, or so I heard, I had got the job through my photograph which had accompanied my application form (I am rather photogenic and am fortunate to be one of those people whom a photograph compliments), for later the chief clerk was overheard to say in a most dreadful drawl, "She's not a bit like her photograph, is she? If only I'd known…" However, for me they were four very happy years working with wonderful people.

It was wonderful to be independent and earning money, although it was really very little. Most of this time I stayed at the hostel until I moved in with my father at a tiny little guest house; it was lovely to have a room next to him. He was such a comforting person, I have never known him say an unkind word about anyone and yet he wasn't a church going person. In fact, he had never been confirmed.

I had many boy friends, girls were comparatively few and far between, and led a very gay life: dancing; playing tennis; moonlight picnics; and all day picnics which we often set off on at about 4.00am so that we could see the sunrise. We had long public holidays when we all went away camping in gangs. On one of these occasions in 1937, I went to a place called Kariba on the Zambesi, which of course now is well-known for the gigantic dam that was built there by the Italians. At this time it was just a spot on the bank of the Zambesi and we girls were the first white women to be seen by many of the natives there. Lions roared around the huts at night and the hyenas laughed, which I found more terrifying and uncanny than anything else. We also had just missed a herd of angry elephants and were shown, with great delight by a native bearer, a huge baobab tree where in its trunk were, still embedded, the bones of a native woman who had been squashed against it. There but for the grace of God went we! We were indeed lucky, for we escaped malaria and sleeping sickness, although we appeared to have been bitten by many mosquitoes and tsetse flies. On our return to Salisbury and just outside the tsetse fly area, we had to drive into a decontamination hut and be thoroughly sprayed: car, belongings, and ourselves.

It was just about this time that I was asked to partner one of the pilots who was passing through on a cruise from Cairo to Cape Town and back. They were all members of 216 Squadron, Royal Air Force from Heliolopis, Egypt and I wasn't very keen as I had heard that airmen were worse than sailors and got through an even greater number of girl friends! However after some deliberation I accepted, for after all hadn't I made my mind up who I was going to marry? Little did I know what a fateful decision that was. At that time I was secretly engaged to John, a boy I had known practically all my life, and it was a foregone conclusion that one day we would eventually be married and live in Salisbury where he was a solicitor. At the time he was away in England for six months and, although I was missing him dreadfully, I thought it wouldn't do any harm to go out for a change with some airmen, although I was quite determined that I would treat them as ships that passed in the night as they would no doubt treat me! The weekend duly arrived and we were presented or so it seemed, to a gay and slightly crazy lot of pilots, both South African and British. We were taken dancing and dining on the Saturday night, and afterwards I went with a party of South Africans to a nightclub called 'The Ace of Spades' about four miles out of town. Here there was more dancing in between bacon and eggs, and during my meal one young British pilot wanted to reach the dance floor and calmly stepped onto the table and down, as that was the quickest way. In doing so, he almost put his foot in my supper. I was more than a little annoyed and thought that the RAF lacked manners as well as much else.

The following day there was a huge picnic at a heavenly spot called Mermaid's Pool and to my horror, I was told that the wing commander in charge of the RAF party had noticed that I had blue eyes. He had thought I would make the ideal partner for his bluest eyed boy, who turned out to be the airman with the large feet who had almost spoilt my eating the night before. I took rather a dim view of this but it was such a perfect day otherwise, so I decided to forgive him and be friends. We had a wonderful time: bathing; sunning; and playing all sorts of jokes, not the least of which was retaliation on my part in the shape of a pint of beer down his neck! I found that his name was Ben and we got on extremely well. I also found to my amazement too that I was beginning to wonder if all the stories I had heard about girls in every airport were true. I began to hope it wasn't, and perhaps I wasn't quite so sure about my boy friend in England! That night we went out to a dinner party together and try as I did, I lost my heart to him in spite of every effort on the part of my mind to tell me not to be so silly. He said he felt the same, but I wondered how often he had said that before!

It was an unhappy night, for they were to leave the next morning. I had promised to see them off and went to bed with a heavy heart, which was full of doubt where as once it had been so sure of its future, and awoke to hear them flying overhead. No, I didn't oversleep, for take-off time had been set for 8.00am and it was only 5.30am. I wondered what he must have been thinking of me, letting him down so soon. I later discovered there had been serious riots on the Copper Belt in Northern Rhodesia and the Vickers Victoria which he was flying, had been loaded with troops. They had left at the crack of dawn and had no farewells as arranged, which perhaps in the acid test of dawn, was a good thing, for they wouldn't have helped to ease my heavy heart. It was awfully hard to concentrate at the office that day, and for nearly two years afterwards! Soon letters began to arrive and we wrote to each other twice a week for two years. During that time I saved every penny I could and in May 1937 had got enough money put aside to travel to England, tourist class, to meet Ben again and make up my mind about marrying him. During the twenty-four months too I had the usual marvellous time, with John constantly by my side. But something niggled at my heart and I *had* to meet Ben again just to be certain that whichever step I took, it would be the right one. It was a difficult time, for I am a sort of sensitive person and I hated hurting anyone. But there it was, and I had somehow to be strong minded.

Those two years had not been uneventful for either of us. Before leaving Egypt on the South African cruise an old Indian had begged to be allowed to tell Ben's fortune. Ben of course would not hear of such a thing, as he thought the whole idea of fortune telling to be quite stupid. Eventually he gave in for the sake of peace, for the old man dogged his footsteps wherever he went. The Indian told him that he was to go on a cruise neither by sea or land, and he would travel far afield. During that journey, he would find a girl with a mole on the side of her face whom he would marry (here, there were shrieks of mirth from the friends with Ben who too didn't believe a word). "Yes," said one, "I bet it will be on the end of her nose." The Indian continued, and said that three days after he had met this girl he was to have a minor accident; about eighteen months after that he would then be involved in a serious one in which many would be killed, but he would be all right, although hurt (more jolly laughter on the part of the onlookers); and after that, he would change his job and get married to this same girl.

~ Chapter Two ~

FIRST POSTING

Do you believe in fortune tellers? Well, I don't know… but every word of it came true. There was me for instance: I have a mole on the left side of my face; three days after leaving Salisbury he wrote-off his undercarriage on an ant heap at Lusaka Airfield (there was no paving in those days, just a flat strip cut out of the African bush); eighteen months later he was involved in a night flying crash in Mersa Matruh when seven out of thirteen were killed; after that he went back to England and changed his job to that of a flying instructor, *and* he did marry me! Thank goodness! For hadn't I chased him seven thousand miles? – or so he likes to tease me. Yes, we were married in 1938, although not without a lot of opposition. My parents were convinced that all RAF pilots were good-for-nothings while his parents were sure that I was something completely wild and only used to talking in tom-tom language, and anyway we were far too young. That was over fifty-four years ago and I know neither of us would have missed that day for anything.

For me, it was in some ways a great struggle going to England on my own. My father was already there at the Coronation as one of the Rhodesian representatives and had gone first class. He and my mother were now divorced, which in those days was a rather horrific thing to do. He had asked me if I wanted any help with my fare, and I had proudly said, "No." However, he was completely shattered when he met me in Southampton and found that I had slummed it and was almost hanging-on to the anchor! "Never mind," he said, "we will go home first class together and make up for it. I have booked your passage." Two months later I had to break the news to him that I was not returning to Rhodesia, but was staying on to marry Ben. It was a terrible wrench as Daddy depended on me so much and we had lived together, as he was a lonely old man and still feeling the separation from my mother. Anyway, he was wonderful about it and didn't try to persuade me to change my mind, but I must admit I cried a lot on my own! Cables from John hadn't helped either, saying he had built a house etc. Sometimes I felt very alone in a strange country, but I simply *had* to have the courage of my convictions.

The next six months were agony in many ways. I had no *real* friends in London, where I was working in Rhodesia House in the Strand. I was so lonely, so cold and, more often than not, I was even hungry. I certainly didn't have enough warm clothes, but I wouldn't admit it. However, the weekends were lovely, for Ben came up to fetch me, he was at Henlow in Bedfordshire, and we would go and stay with friends or his parents in Buckinghamshire. But Sunday evening seemed to come around so quickly. Eventually I gave up my job in Rhodesia House and went down to Devon to my aunt and uncle where I stayed until we were married in St George's, Hanover Square, on 2nd April 1938. We had wanted to be married in a tiny church near Upavon in Wiltshire where we would have had about ten guests, but Ben's mother wanted a large wedding and I am afraid, that is what we had! We were upset at the time, but I think we are glad now. The High Commissioner for South Rhodesia gave me away, and I think that I only knew five people at my own wedding among the three hundred guests. In fact, I had not met one of my bridesmaids until the night before. I had wanted a full skirted romantic wedding dress. But no, I had to have a classic one that cost the earth! It was at such times I missed not having my own parents to discuss things with, and also my girl friends who would advise. Granny Boult meant well, and I don't mean that nastily, but she just hadn't had a daughter and wasn't 'with it' as my children would say these days!

The best wedding present I had, which doubled my happiness, was that fate had stepped in and my berth on the ship returning to South Africa had been taken by a very wonderful person who became my stepmother! She and my father had known each other for years but had never been thrown together. She made my father extremely happy and to whom I shall be eternally grateful.

We had a wonderful honeymoon, motoring along the south coast of England stopping where we felt inclined and returning via north Cornwall and the Rhonda Valley to Hereford and Kenley, where Ben was to be adjutant of 615 Squadron. We were returning early as his name had been drawn out of a hat to do Easter duties. One heavenly day during our honeymoon, we decided to take a picnic lunch and find a quiet secluded spot. This we managed to do almost at Land's End, and settled down to eat wondering why the place was so deserted when we had seen a lot of cars further along the road. However, the silence was soon shattered by a large explosion, for we had not noticed the red flags and there was blasting all around! Obviously we only had eyes for each other.

On our return to Kenley, we had to find somewhere to live. My introduction to the Service had been of the severest kind, as on the day before we were married I had to sit outside an Air Ministry office in the car for four and a half hours (like Peter Rabbit under the basket!). I have found that service life has been the same ever since and, more often than not, the people in the postings branch are unable to make up their minds for long! History will reveal what I mean. Yes, on that day previous to our meeting in church, we were posted *three* times: to Kenley, to Filton, and then back to Kenley. We stayed the first night in the Surrey Hills Hotel (later bombed and erased from the earth's surface together with the morning cup of tea which we ordered and which never arrived!) and then were kindly lent a house while its occupiers were away on leave. I was petrified of the gas cooker and even more frightened of the maid, for I had never had a white servant in my life and found it quite unnatural after always having Africans. To this day I never really feel at ease when waited upon by someone of my own race.

The search for somewhere to live began that day and that search was to continue in the same way off and on, for almost twenty-one years with varying success. We went into a hundred houses all round Kenley, Purley and Caterham and eventually asked the owner of one which had 'For Sale' outside it, if she would consider letting it instead. She said she might, only she had nowhere to put her furniture. We almost fell upon her neck and said that we would do her a great favour and look after it for her. She was charming and agreed. Within ten days we were settled in 'Windy' which was in bad need of redecoration. Ben made some enquires as to how long we would be with the Squadron, and was told *at least* two years but probably longer. So we set to work painting and digging a garden out of solid chalk, innocents that we were, for eight months later we were posted! A very strange thing happened years later in 1960, I met the owner of Windy again at a coffee morning in Accra, Ghana.

During that eight months, although we had met a lot of very nice people, most of them were soon to be killed in the Battle of Britain. Once again I was to be initiated into the uncertainty of a service wife's life when the telephone rang one night and the Squadron was ordered to move to an unspecified destination. This was at the time of the Munich Crisis when war seemed to be imminent. Ben could tell me nothing of course, or if he could, he wouldn't naturally, and that is the way we have continued all our life. It was agreed that I should shut up the house and go to my mother who was then in Bournemouth, and Ben would ring me when he could from wherever he was. Perhaps it doesn't sound much now, but at the time it was grim and seemed as if the world was coming to an end. However the following day, after he had left before dawn and I had heard the planes take-off, I packed a suitcase, put the dog in the car and drove off to Dorset. That night he rang me from just up the road as it were, as the Squadron was at Old Sarum! The flap was soon over, and we all returned to Kenley.

Then there followed the Squadron camp at Thorney Island. 61 Squadron was an auxiliary squadron and we had a fortnight's camp every year. The ground crews travelled by lorry and I drove my car to Emsworth, where I stayed near my husband, picnicking en route, and overtaking and being overtaken by the convoy – waving frantically at them each time. When we left Kenley shortly after this, Ben was presented with a little silver beer mug and my name was coupled with his 'For boosting the morale of the troops'! That indeed was wonderful repayment for such a few gestures of friendliness on my part, and ranks among my greatest treasures.

From Kenley to Upavon and into another little bungalow, 'St Patrick's'. Here the greatest event of our life so far was to take place, for we became the proud parents of a son, Peter. Those halcyon days of peace were not to last long, for six weeks after he was born, Hitler marched on Poland and war was declared.

Well do I remember that Sunday when we heard the fateful announcement, and well do I remember too the words of our best man when he turned to me and said, "One thing I pray and that is that this war will not harm you both and your wee son." Words that mean even more perhaps now, for he was shortly to be killed on the second sortie the Defiants made when they were ruthlessly all shot down. However, we soon cheered up and made fun of having to put up blackout curtains etc and thought for the next few months that the war was really phoney as nothing seemed to be happening – at least to us.

We moved house again into a lovely double storied building, namely 'Dormy Cottage'. We had a lot of fun over this move, for we didn't tell my mother-in-law anything about it, but when she came to stay we asked her if she would mind if we just popped into see some people for a moment. You can imagine her surprise when the front door was opened by our 'nanny'. I think that was to be the first and only time that the two grannies were to meet, for my mother had come up for Peter's christening in the little church at Upavon, and then the war was to send us all on our different ways.

There were odd nights which we spent when Ben would be giving flying instruction, sometimes completely through the night. At other times we would sit up until about midnight trying to keep awake, usually doing jigsaw puzzles until it was time for him to leave for his detail, and then being told that the flying would be cancelled for the weather had clamped, and we would then fall into bed exhausted through waiting. On other evenings, I would drive up to the flight with Horlicks etc to keep the crews awake, although the drink was supposed to be good for sleep! On yet another night Ben did a Charlie Chaplin act, for I saw him cross the airfield edge to cancel night flying silhouetted against the flares, and then suddenly disappear. He had fallen down a disused oil pit! That was one battle dress that was never used again.

The winter of 1940 came and was a terribly hard one. Frozen rain making everything beautiful but doing untold damage, splitting trees and telegraph poles like matchwood and in a way, being a grim forerunner of things to come much later on. But we somehow enjoyed it, and drip trays made wonderful toboggans down the Upavon slopes.

Spring and summer came, with Dunkirk as a grim reminder that the war was well and truly on. I can remember sitting Peter in his pram at the edge of the garden to watch the unshaven and weary soldiers being driven past, so that one day he would be able to say he had watched them, although he wouldn't actually remember it. I felt that this was history indeed.

A lot of our friends at this time were managing to leave Training Command and become fighter pilots. Of course Ben had a go at convincing, or trying to, the Air Ministry that he was *the* born fighter pilot, but he was told in no uncertain way that he had to get back to his instructing and, what was more, he would be leaving for Canada in thirty-six hours time to do so! Imagine my surprise when the telephone rang and he calmly said, "Darling, can you be ready to go to Canada tomorrow afternoon?" "Yes," said I, and immediately rang a good friend of mine, asked her if she would look after the baby, got in touch with Pickfords and then Granny, and I was set too. We managed somehow, although in the middle of it, Ben rang again to say that now it was to be Kenya and the day after… Having packed everything we decided to stay the extra day at the local pub. Ben came back and said that all the luggage was to go to Southampton and we might or might not be allowed to go together. It was a case of wait and see, and wait we did, for *six* weeks later we sailed for Rhodesia not from Southampton, but from Liverpool!

Being rather rash and the trains so crowded, we decided to hire a car and be driven to Liverpool and there spend one last night in the lap of luxury, for we knew not what the future would hold and were determined to part with a lovely memory. However, arriving at Liverpool we found that all the hotels had been commandeered and that accommodation was difficult in the extreme. Eventually we managed to find one single room with one single, much buckled, iron bedstead in it on the sixth floor of the Imperial Hotel – and no lift! Peter and I cried all the way up those flights! Having sorted ourselves a little we thought a cup of tea and some bread and butter would be nice. This we managed to acquire downstairs, with the bread as thickly cut as I have ever seen it, "for the Air Force boys liked it that way." To bed with no theatre or private bathroom as we had planned, but instead a view over the roof tops and Peter sleeping in the bottom drawer of a dressing table.

The next day was a nightmare, for everything was so disorganised. The first thing was to try to find out whether or not I was travelling, but were told that we would only know this at the very last hour, for if the reserved cabins for Ministry officials were not occupied the wives would then be allowed to travel. Peter of course was very upset and spent the morning in tears. Eventually Ben got him to sleep and we decided to take him in his carrycot over to the Adelphi where we had a cup of coffee. We had coffee in the dining room, for it was the quietest place we could find. At least it was for ten minutes, for then two men armed with blowlamps and hammers came in to do the central heating pipes. However, the afternoon came eventually, and the evening brought the good news that I could go too. We had armed ourselves with a tuck box full of Heinz baby foods, so Peter was at least catered for. We found that we were to travel in first class, in luxury just when Britain seemed to be loosing the war. When we were winning it several years later, we were to travel in complete bedlam, but more of that later.

~ Chapter Three ~

RETURN TO AFRICA

We left at sunset to the strains of 'Roll out the barrel' and accompanied by one destroyer. We were on board the Windsor Castle and destined for the Elementary Flying Training School (EFTS) at Guinea Fowl, South Rhodesia. We slept well that night feeling safe in the care of the Royal Navy, but imagine our surprise when we awoke the next morning to find we were going solo! Soon we arrived at St Vincent in the Cape Verde Islands and it was wonderful to see all the lights, for everything in England had then been blacked out for almost a year. Peter celebrated his first birthday here and we all enjoyed his party in spite of the fact that some kind soul had circulated a rumour that half the German submarine fleet were waiting outside, to torpedo us the moment we showed our nose in the Atlantic. Of course we *knew* it was only a rumour, but where there's smoke there's fire some said and, although we laughed it off, it left a jingling in our tummies!

However, we crept out unnoticed, or so it appeared, for all went well and we reached Ascension Island in due course and here the inhabitants came out in a small boat and bought up everything in the barber's shop. We were told that the sea teamed with small black fish about a foot long, that would devour anything quicker than the eye could see. To prove this the airmen on board caught some, put them in a canvas swimming bath and then threw in chunks of steak. It was quite true! We then believed everything we were told about them, being even more harmful than sharks. It was incredible to see huge chunks of meat disappear as if they had been bread crumbs.

On with the voyage: hot days and nights; schools of porpoises; lots of flying fish; and lovely phosphorescence at night. It all seemed very far removed from the war, with first class service and food no one would have thought that at that time Britain was apparently losing the Battle of the Atlantic or that, on her next voyage out to Africa, the Windsor Castle would be sunk… Later we reached St Helena and here there were shore visits and much selling of lace etc on deck. Some airman left a note at the local post office addressed to Adolf Hitler, 'To await arrival' – shades of Napoleon Bonaparte.

Cape Town, and Table Mountain really did us proud, for it was covered with a gorgeous table cloth. I had an aunt who lived about forty miles outside the city and Ben got us permission to telephone her. Although in bed with flu, she nevertheless got up and drove in just to have about ten minutes with us at the station, and in order to see her grand-nephew that she had heard so much about. True to form, we were told that we would not be disembarking until the next day, but someone somewhere changed their minds and we were all off the ship within four hours. Unfortunately, I had left a lovely silver and enamel powder flapjack on the cabin dressing table. Although I wrote to the company about it the following day and posted the letter from the train, of course it was never found. To me it was a great loss, but I suppose it was a very petty thing to worry about when people were losing their lives and homes elsewhere daily.

We all piled on to a troop train and we rigged up one of the bunks as a cot and play pen for Peter, who was by now quite used to strange conditions. He had often been tethered to a railing on the ship like a goat, while we exercised ourselves! When he became hot and dirty, as we all did when travelling through the Karoo Desert, we simply let him sit in the washbasin and play like a great Buddha – he was certainly the cleanest person on that train! Four days later we arrived at Gwelo and I suppose to most people it must have been rather a shock, but of course to me it was heaven. Absolutely so, for my father and stepmother had travelled down from Salisbury to greet us.

We settled into Meikles Hotel, once known as a white elephant, but one that certainly developed into a gold mine for the owner, once the Royal Air Force arrived! After a few weeks we decided that we simply couldn't afford it any longer, and anyway it was fourteen miles from the camp. With flying starting at 4.30am it was too much of a good thing, so we searched for and found some accommodation on a farm near the EFTS which consisted of two rondavels joined by a veranda. Here we went into the main house for meals and down the garden path for other things!

All went well for several months until one day a large mamba crossed my path and was bent on reclining in the thatch of our bedroom roof. A day later another was dangling happily from a tree above the pram keeping our son and heir quiet with its fascinating antics. I grabbed the pram, ran and shouted for help which duly came in the shape of the farmer, who disposed of the reptile and almost gave me the impression he couldn't understand what all the fuss was about. However, I was very shaken and we then moved once more, this time into a cheaper hotel in Gwelo. Every time I wanted to grumble, at 4.00am when I sat up in bed and cleaned Ben's buttons, I thought of the snakes and was quite happy. We made friends with a lot of people here and among them some at Shabani, where we visited the asbestos mines.

Things were just beginning to settle down when of course, we were posted to Salisbury and the Rhodesian Air Training Group HQ! We had bought a wonderful(?) old Vauxhall car which rattled like a tin can and had a minus number of brakes, no tools and no spare tyre – and went by the name of 'Sally Salvage'. Well of course Ben had to fly to Salisbury and someone had to drive the car from A to B – and that someone was *me*. I heard of a flight sergeant who wanted a free trip to the capital, but he never turned up on the morning of departure. I suppose he had done a recce the night before, seen the car, and decided that the free trip could wait. Nothing daunted, Peter and I, and a large bull-mastiff dog called Pim, embarked at about 7.00am. With a revolver to comfort me, we set sail quite happily with two hundred miles of Africa between me and my destination. The roads were concrete stripped all the way, which meant one had to concentrate. It was rather like driving along a railway line: when one met another car, you each gave way keeping the right wheels on a strip and the others in a ditch, rut, corrugations or, if you were lucky, a smooth bit of African soil. However, we reached Salisbury that evening, and apart from seeing strips before the eye for about twenty-four hours, no harm was done.

We had booked accommodation in an annex to a well-known boarding house, but after a few weeks managed to find a house about six miles out of town. It was a very nice bungalow and we were very happy especially when our wee daughter Penelope appeared on the scene. We had one or two amusing incidents though. One of them was not really so funny, as I was bitten hard and in a very unfriendly manner in the seat by Pim, our dog, who had developed into a huge beast with a thirty-six inch chest measurement. Ben had flown to Cape Town and back in a Harvard, taking the then Prime Minister of South Rhodesia, Sir Godfrey Huggins, to meet that great man General Smuts to talk over the maize (or mielie) famine. While he was away Pim got completely out of hand and after taking a chunk out of me, was sent to kennels to await the return of the Lord and Master. Incidentally, Ben had the great honour while he was away of having tea at Groote Schuur, the home of the South African Prime Minister.

On Ben's return Pim was duly returned to store but wasn't really safe, so was given to a mounted policeman friend of ours who said he was just the sort of dog he wanted. The policeman took him out into the veldt and on the first night, Pim had scattered all the pie-dogs within miles. Not being satisfied with that, he then started on the native piccaninnies. This wasn't good enough for an officer of the law, so back Pim came. Our original donor then said he would have him but, although he was an exceptionally strong man, found that he was unable to control the dog. Eventually the dog had to be shot, which was a very sad ending to a beautiful beast who never need have gone that way if it hadn't been for the fact that while Ben was flying, the airmen on the ground had taught him to fight.

A slightly lighter thing happened just when we were about to move into our first married quarter. We had kept chickens in the bungalow and were fattening them up for a house warming in the next house. The day before we left 'Highlands' for official lodgings, we looked at the chickens and decided that they would make a good meal and would have them killed the following morning; the cookboy could then bring them with him to the new house. Imagine our dismay when, with the early morning tea, we were greeted with, "Master, all hookoos gone." Someone else had been watching them too, for during the night the lot, about five in all, had been stolen. Although the chicken run door was locked, it had been no deterrent, for a hole had been dug under the netting!

We shared our quarter for about a month with a charming wing commander and his equally charming wife, and then off they went to some other part of the world. In the meantime, we had become firm friends and remain so to this day. They had a son about the same age (in fact a twin all bar two days) as Peter, and he was a brilliant child who at three could recite the alphabet and numerous nursery rhymes while my blond, beautiful and rather fat wee son couldn't do a thing. My heart sank, and I wondered what would become of him. In fact the two boys much later, were at the same public school together and were equal in most things, except that Chris later went to university while Peter got a scholarship to Cranwell.

After we had been revelling in the luxury of a quarter for about three months, naturally Ben was posted! Those three months had been the greatest fun though, and also quite amusing. One incident that springs to mind was the day we decided to light a fire and the smoke just came out into the sitting room. We duly reported it, and the clerk of works rolled up to see what was the matter. Laying flat on his back in the fireplace, he saw the blue sky above and said we were imagining things. So we tried again, but this time he saw for himself that the smoke really did come down instead of go up. Later he discovered that some twit of a native builder had placed a sheet of glass across the chimney half way up! We had the most wonderful cookboy here too, about three feet high who wore a chef's hat about two feet tall. He adored having people to dinner, and when at first I said rather tremulously, "Six extra I'm afraid tonight George." He would say, "Oh missus, only six." However, he had his answer when one night we brought twenty-seven people back for bacon and eggs after a dance. George didn't turn a hair!

Eventually the day came to move. Housing was a terrible problem: we moved into rooms for a few weeks; then someone lent us a flat for a few weeks; then into a house for two months, which was really blissful; then back into another set of rooms; and so it went on. Ben in the meantime was instructing once more, and his work with Greek pupils earned him the Royal Hellenic Air Force Cross, of which we are all very proud. The actual award and citation reached us eleven years later having been via the Far East! He had also been awarded the Air Force Cross (AFC) the year before, so we had two really good parties which took our minds off the moving for several hours! The day did dawn when we had to move out of a borrowed flat and we just hadn't been able to find anywhere to stay. I'm ashamed to say of my countrymen that in many homes and boarding houses, people with children were not welcome. The population was so swollen that the residents could afford to be choosy.

Ben went to the air officer commander and asked permission for myself and the two children to be allowed to live with him in his bachelor CO's flat out at Norton, the Rhodesian Central Flying School of which he was to be the commanding officer. This station was rather fun, for Ben had helped to choose the site and place the buildings, and it was with great pride that he took over command. The flat was most awfully nice and consisted of two large rooms and a bathroom etc with a veranda running along the front. The children had their meals in the flat and I went over to the mess, to the Ladies' Room, to join Ben for mine. We played a lot of tennis in between the hard work, and Sunday lunch sessions over Pimm's after church parade became quite the thing.

Often during the rainy season we would have several extra people for the night, for the Hunyani River between us and Salisbury would rise and the low level bridge would become unusable. We fitted them in somehow, and it was all great fun. We also had one holiday down in Natal too, which was wonderful after the children had got over several days of gippy tummy and sickness caused from the change of altitude and food (Rhodesia is five thousand feet above sea level). On the return journey, which was four days in a train, we must have spread measles unknowingly throughout the whole of the southern part of Africa. When we got on the train at Durban, Peter was sick again (the joys of being a mother!) but naturally enough, I just thought he had eaten something. However, it continued for the rest of the trip on and off, and the day after we arrived back on the camp he was covered with a rash; and ten days after that, so was I! Penny and Ben, who had been confined in the same compartment with us, never got a thing!

All this time we had been watching our married quarter grow. Then the day came to take it over and, believe it or not, as Ben dipped his pen into the ink-well to sign the necessary papers, the telephone rang and a kind voice at the other end said, "I thought you might like to know that you have been posted home next month!" So that was that. Our second in command moved in instead and I started packing. For some reason better known to themselves, Ben and I had to travel separately for security reasons which seemed ridiculous when we later waited three months together near Durban for a ship to take us back to England. Anyway, I travelled down to Natal with the two children and a week later met Ben on the platform in Durban. We then went out to Umkomaas, where we and many others were to await orders. This three months could have been a wonderful holiday, but it was really a very frustrating time, for each day we thought we would embark and, as each day went by, the boys got more and more anxious to get home and win the war.

As it was, Ben had an exciting experience, for he was nearly arrested for wearing a Distinguished Flying Cross (DFC) upside down and *after* the AFC. The police in Durban thought for an hour or so that they had really got their man, for they were looking for a bogus wing commander. But after much talking and producing of documents, Ben was able to prove that it was the Greek AFC that he was wearing, which was exactly like the DFC only upside down – the ribbon has since been changed. Anyway, it was a cause for drinks all round and later he was able to claim another free beer…

The days were hot and sticky and we spent as much time as possible in the gorgeous sea pool which was built into the rocks so that the sea broke over them into the swimming bath which enabled it to have fresh water daily – it also prevented the sharks from entering.

Penny was just about thirteen months old then and, poor child, rather miserable, for she had been moved from pillar to post and was thoroughly upset. We made friends with another air force couple who had a son the same age. Between us, we shared a nanny whom I can see to this day wheeling two yelling children up the steep incline from the beach. Each child was armed with a bunch of bananas, which we knew they could devour peacefully once they were out of sight of their respective mamas – but they never departed without making themselves heard in no uncertain manner.

~ Chapter Four ~

BACK TO WAR

At last the day came when we were to leave. We were told that we were to board the Empress of Scotland, once the Empress of Japan, and would only be allowed two suitcases: one for the cabin with tropical clothes; and one for the hold with winter clothes, for we would be arriving in England at the end of February. Much packing and sorting out was needed, but once we were on board I saw the reason for this: eight hundred women and children, thousands of troops, and the minimum of space per person. However, we felt we were truly lucky to be travelling with our husbands and discovered later that we were the last bunch of wives to do so. The two children and myself were in a four berth cabin converted to make room somehow for fourteen of us, and eight of those children were under the age of six! I was allotted two bunks and when we all assembled, we had a conference and decided that no one must be sea sick, for surely everyone would then follow suit. This was awfully difficult for me, for I am one of the world's worst sailors. But I couldn't let the side down and, for the first and last time in my life, I was *not* sea sick, although I used to sleep with Penny on my tummy at night to keep it steady. How I managed such self control I do not know, but it worked.

Whenever we moved we had to carry lifebelts (in my case three!) and a 'panic bag' which contained all the things one might want if we should be torpedoed. Things such as calamine lotion for sunburn, head coverings, and then jerseys etc for cold weather. There were no chairs on deck and we all sat on the floor. Meals were at 7.30am, 11.30am lunch and 5.30pm supper, and that was that. At night we sat in the corridors outside our cabins. We had boat drill twice a day but there was no need to panic we were told, for the sister ship had taken twenty minutes to sink! Ben decided that being a fairly little chap and having a bunk in a hold with five hundred others, it just wouldn't be worth being killed in the rush to get out. So he kept a bottle of brandy under his pillow which he was going to consume steadily in the case of emergency and just fall into oblivion and go down with the ship knowing nothing about it. He had meals at different times to myself and the children, and was also on submarine watch, so I just never saw him. My cabin was down five flights of stairs and each time I managed to get up on deck, sure enough, one of the infants would say, "Potty, Mummy." So down we would go, panic bag and all – and then up aloft again probably arriving just in time to have to descend again for boat drill.

We stayed outside Cape Town for a day and a half. Of course I was not allowed to get in touch with my mother, who was then living just outside the city and of course, she had no idea which ship I was on or if I had even left Durban… That was forty-nine years ago and I never saw her for seventeen years. Some of the wives decided that after four days journey from Durban they had had enough and that conditions were so awful that they would go ashore and wait until after the war – it takes all sorts doesn't it?! We sailed on up the west coast of Africa and the days went by somehow. So did the nights, which were unbearable at times for all portholes were battened down and the ship seemed to be airless. No one was allowed on deck, for someone had abused the privilege and had been seen lighting a cigarette. Off Freetown we were greeted by a flying boat and it was the most terrific thrill, we really felt safe for a few hours. When it began to get cool someone rang a bell and alphabetically we went down into the baggage room to swap suitcases. Of course, when I arrived to collect mine, there was no sign of it anywhere… It had been put on the wrong ship and what was more, we never did see it again! For a few days I was in a predicament for no one really had any warm clothes to spare when we were only allowed such a little luggage, but someone had knitting wool and, between two wonderful airmen's wives and myself, we knitted the children two jerseys each. Another wife gave me a viyella blouse and a sailor gave me a sheepskin jerkin! That was the top half catered for. The ship's hospital then kindly gave me a couple of grey blankets and, together with some other wives who helped with the stitching, I made the children battle dresses! I was lent a pair of corduroy trousers and that was how we eventually landed in England which was rather sad after having bought complete new winter outfits in Africa, at great expense, for the three of us!

Two days from England we had a scare, sirens in every direction and we all assembled in our cabins. I remember strapping the potty on to the side of my panic bag, for I was sure it would be much needed. With an unidentified aircraft above, we had a few minutes of real fright, but luckily the cloud base was very low and there was a terrific storm in the offing – the gods were on our side. I must say *everyone* behaved magnificently.

We landed at Liverpool and it was tragic to see all the signs of the bombing. Thoughts went through my mind of when I was last there three years ago with only one child, things seemed comparatively peaceful then with the exception of the workman with his blowlamp! Then too we had set out on a luxury cruise, but this time in spite of the war going so well for the Allies, we had really travelled in dreadful conditions. The main thing was that we had arrived safely and all together. I shall always remember how helpful and cheerful *everyone* on that ship was, none of the moaning and groaning one gets from fellow passengers in peacetime.

We travelled by troop train to London and had to disembark at Olympia, for the other station where our arrival had been planned had been bombed. We were going to Medmenham in Buckinghamshire to Ben's father and stepmother, but discovered that the only train was one leaving at about 9.00pm arriving at about 10.30pm due to all sorts of delays. So there was nothing for it but to wait on the platform at Paddington. Several people who saw us in our peculiar garb offered to help or direct us, thinking we were refugees. Eventually we left, and half an hour after our departure the platform was no more, for Hitler had had one final shot at us. We were received with open arms as you can imagine, but it had all been rather too much for Peter who showed his relief at arriving safely at our destination by being sick all over the drawing room carpet!

The next day we slept late and then I left the children with my stepmother-in-law and went up to London to buy clothes – lovely thought. Ben too had to visit the Air Ministry after a few days, and once more only just managed to escape arrest due to the Greek AFC, for he was stopped by two constables on Paddington platform and asked to, "Step aside for a moment please." All rather difficult, for when they asked him for his unit, of course he said he hadn't one as he was just on his way to the Air Ministry to see where he was off to. He also had no 1369 (identity card) as he had been told that the Air Ministry would issue him with a new one etc... However, he won the day and drinks were had all round. He was eventually posted to Bicester to qualify on Mosquitoes prior to taking over a squadron, but before this we had to find somewhere for me to live. We decided on Hereford as I had an aunt there. After several various sorties into different guest houses, we found a sweet little cottage from which the agent proudly said one could view seven counties on a clear day. He didn't stress the fact that there was no electric light; a ram that pumped water very spasmodically; that it was three quarters of a mile from the nearest bus stop; and *only* five and a half guineas per week. However, we were desperate and settled in.

Ben went off for his training, but was heartbroken when a few weeks later he was posted to Finmere and switched to Mitchells. Anyway, eventually he became devoted to these aircraft and was given command of 180 Squadron which was stationed at Dunsfold in Sussex. They were medium bombers and Granny and I used to spend several really uncomfortable evenings listening to the radio and the announcement that, "One of our Mitchells didn't return." Ben used to ring often, but we never made a rule about telephone calls. When he did ring we had a code in the shape of, "Did you see Philip today?" If he said, "Yes," then I knew he had been on a sortie. I also had one good reply, I thought, to several dear old ladies who smarmed over me and said, "My dear, how dreadful for you having a husband on bombers. You must be worried to death." "Oh no!" replied I, "Not at all. If anything happens to him I can go home to Africa first class on the insurance." I couldn't bear being sympathised with by people who had nothing to lose and anyway were making a packet out of the RAF and the unfortunate wives of its pilots.

D-Day came with all its excitement, wonderings and worryings. As usual the battery to our wireless always failed at the crucial moment, so that we used to have to rush to the gardener's cottage nearby and listen to the news. Peter was already five years old then and was for his age, rather serious. Indeed he had had a lot to think about and perhaps a lot of it was summed up in a remark he made when we travelled in a bus from Reading to Medmenham where he saw the luggage shelves above the passengers heads, "Mummy," he said, "why do people sleep in buses in England?" So much for the Empress of Scotland!

Just as Peter was five years old, in fact at 1.00am on the 25th July 1944, the telephone rang. I heard it in my sleep and was terrified – frightened for two reasons: one, because it never rang at night and I *felt* it must be important; and secondly, because I thought I would never get there before it stopped ringing.

How ashamed I am of all the time I have wasted. How very much that it strikes me when every Sunday in church I pray for 'time for amendment of life'. Please God that I may have time to do some of those things I ought to have done for so long…

So much has happened since I wrote the preceding pages, almost three precious years have passed! Anyway, I can still hear the ring of that telephone in 1944 and of course, I did get there in time to answer it. When I lifted the receiver and managed to collect enough breath to say, "Hello," a charming voice at the other end said, "This is the duty officer, RAF Tangmere. We thought you would like to know that your husband has crash landed here and is in hospital at St Richard's, Chichester. He is wounded but will be all right. If you would like to hear further details I suggest you speak to the duty MO." I believe I thanked him. I did in my heart anyway, but I was too shocked, and yet relieved, to say much. I then put a call through to the medical officer who was very nice, but conveyed almost as much to me as does a hospital sister when one rings up to enquire of a friend, "Quite comfortable," which of course means absolutely nothing! However, he did tell me that Ben had been wounded in the eye, arm and leg and that I should go down to see him as soon as I could. *That* left enough food for thought anyway. I thanked him and told him that I would have to arrange for someone to come and look after the children before I could get down to see him. He promised to give Ben my love and tell him what I was doing. Then I can remember sitting at the end of Granny's bed and telling her all about it. We thought it would be a good thing if I rang Ben's cousin Margaret Stead, herself a war widow, and ask her to come for a day or two while I went down to Chichester. My head was too full of thoughts to allow me to sleep much more that night. Would he be disfigured forever? Would he be blind? Would he be crippled etc? In the morning the post girl arrived and I can remember her saying as she handed me a telegram, "I'm afraid it's not good news M'am," but I was able to tell her that I had heard already. In one way I was thankful that for me, for the time being, the war was 'over'. No more wondering if Ben was on a raid. No more heart stopping when I heard on the radio, "One of our Mitchells is missing." That much I was very thankful for.

Margaret was an absolute brick. She arrived that evening and the following morning I set off. The trains were absolutely full of course, and I sat on my suitcase in the corridor between Gloucester and London. I then did the same all the way down to Chichester, a journey which seemed to take ages and involved so many changes. Eventually, I did arrive at the hospital and was ushered into Ben's private ward. My heart was too full to speak and he was not allowed to move. He had even to be fed, for the eye was very badly damaged. In fact the whole cheek appeared to be vastly swollen and the eye quite out of place.

The specialists were debating whether or not to remove the eye and a chance remark made by Ben made up their minds for them. He had heard and recognised his navigator's footsteps in the corridor and when they stopped at the door Ben said, "Just a minute Paddy," where upon the doctors thought he had seen Paddy and, as there must be some sight in the eye, they decided to leave it! In the end, Ben did have a little indirect vision but almost the whole of the retina had been shot away. This meant that he had to teach himself to focus all over again. At first it was pathetic to see him try to pour water into a glass, he missed it time after time but being the person he is, conquered all this and learnt to shoot off the left shoulder. Above all I think, we as a family have always admired his wonderful courage and determination to overcome his affliction and the way in which he never grumbles or complains. A true example to us all.

Ben was in hospital for six weeks. The arm and the knee healed and it was a miracle the way the flak had passed right through both limbs and had not touched or damaged a muscle! A miracle indeed, as was the whole episode. It took sometime before I got the complete story, and then it was not from my husband but from the co-pilots of the Squadron, whom the padre took me to meet after one of my visits to St Richard's. They told me that Ben had been leading one of the boxes of four Mitchells that was detailed to bomb Caen and when he was over the target, the mechanism jammed and his bombs would not come away. He made another two runs in the face of very heavy flak and then, as his co-pilot was killed beside him, he was hit in the face, arm and leg. There was nothing for it, but to turn for home. He wondered if he would make it, but over the Channel the navigator gave a kick at the bombs which then fell into the sea. Otherwise, Ben was going to give the order to jump and then face his aircraft for Germany before he jumped himself. However, as the bombs did come away he decided to make for Tangmere knowing that he would never make base, and there crash landed safely. The miracle was that all his instruments had been shot away except for the airspeed indicator which was vital! The Almighty certainly had a hand in the events of the day. The contrast to all this was that as Ben was carried out of the aircraft and laid on a stretcher, he remembers putting his gold pencil, one that I had given him, on his tummy and folded his hands over it, but when he awoke in hospital it had gone! How mean can you get?

At the end of six weeks he came home on sick leave and the first thing that happened was that Penny fell out of her cot and hurt her back! We had to take her to be X-rayed and nothing appeared to be damaged, but for weeks she had a very stiff back and neck and when she turned to listen to one, she had to turn her whole body and not just her head. Eventually it righted itself and in due course too, the leave came to an end and Ben had to report for duty again – but they said he would never fly again. There they were quite wrong and had not taken into account Ben's love of the air and his great determination. He managed to persuade someone to let him try to fly again at Swanton Morley, where he succeeded in passing out as completely competent. "Oh! Yes," they said, "maybe by day but *not* at night." That's just where they were wrong, because before long he had been tested again at night and was declared fit and back to standard.

For a while, Ben was attached to Blackbush and I had moved into a house at Ross-on-Wye. After a while he was sent to HQ 2 Group Second Tactical Air Force, Germany to be under Basil Embery as his wing commander Ops, and was unable to get home for Christmas. However, I did get a wonderful surprise, for a few days after Christmas I got a telegram saying that he was to go on the Army course at Camberley from the middle of January. I let the house and we all lived at the 'Prior's Kitchen' for six months. I can remember one day Ben being almost mobbed when he brought a met balloon home for the children. There were no balloons in the shops during the war, or very few, and it caused great excitement. I remember too another occasion when he was almost mobbed! This time it was when he was going down in a lift in Harrods clutching about six toilet rolls, unwrapped and tied together with string! "Where did you get them," he was asked over and over again, for they too were very hard to come by at times!

It was while we were at Camberley too that the first thousand bomber raids took place on Germany. I can well remember seeing an endless stream of aircraft droning overhead for what seemed hours, and then seeing them on the return journey while others were still on their way out. Some of those returning were obviously damaged and there were also a few ominous spaces between them. My heart was so thankful as I at least had my man safe, if not wholly sound, with me and had nothing for the moment to fear.

It was here too that one evening I stepped out of my bath and had a very dizzy attack which lasted for some hours. I often wonder, if I had known then that that was the beginning of many years of the same attacks, would I have had the courage to face up to them? I am sure I would have, for the Almighty always gives one strength to cope with the most impossible situations. I believe more than anything that one is never tested more than one's strength, although that *is* hard to believe at times! However, I went to see a doctor and when I complained that I was tired he said, "My dear, everyone in England is tired," in such a way that I felt very small and that I would never tell my thoughts to a doctor again. Perhaps that is one reason why I always hold back, and am such an obstinate being and won't give in. I think it is a kind of inferiority streak I have in me, one of being afraid of being thought of as a 'sissy'. All I do know for certain is that I would never have been able to cope with life if it hadn't been for the wonderful love, thoughtfulness and above all, understanding of my most precious family. I have never ceased to wonder why they haven't tired of me long ago!

The Camberley course duly ended with a flourish, for we went to the Summer Ball which was a lovely affair. One to be remembered always. Ben went back to 2 Group and was stationed in Brussels where he celebrated VE Day with bottles of champagne, while the children and I returned to Ross-on-Wye and our many chores. I celebrated VE Day by going to bed early and sharing my double bed with Peter and Penny, who were afraid of the fireworks and the noise of the singing soldiers who passed our house, full of spirits on their way back to camp! Chores…Yes, well I remember Peter making the early morning tea for me at the age of five and a half, admittedly in my bedroom. Better even do I remember going into the playroom one morning during the holidays when it was his job to clear out the fireplace each day, and hearing him say to himself, "Wow! I shall be glad when school starts again and my chores are finished!" No wonder he has been such a wonderful son, the best any one can wish for: such a companion; so understanding; and such a *man*. He was at kindergarten school then and loved it, except for the dancing classes when his obstinate streak came out. His report said, "Peter must learn to dance when he is told and not just when he feels like it."

Penny was at another kindergarten and proving to everyone that she was most obstinate too, but how wonderful she turned out to be. A better and more loving daughter no one could wish for. No one could have been more unselfish later when I was ill, but more of that in due course.

During this time of living alone I became really ill and had to close the house and go down to stay with my aunt in Devon. Ben managed to get over from Brussels to take me to a head and brain specialist, but we will gloss over that rather dreary time. Sufficient to say that we were somewhat shattered when we discovered that I had to wait for my appointment in the waiting room of a lunatic asylum, amongst people counting their thumbs! However, eventually I was seen and the specialist was shattered that I should have been asked to go there. We became firm friends and later I used to visit her at her rooms in Bristol every three months.

Finally the glorious day came when Ben was posted back to England, to Hullavington which was the Empire Central Flying School. We had more accommodation troubles and for a time shared a vicarage in Chippenham, but it wasn't a great success. It had only one kitchen and the vicar's wife wanted me to be clear of it during meal hours which meant we had to have our meals at the most peculiar times. She didn't like children either, and I was allowed to have only one with me, so I left Peter at Starcross with my aunt, which he hated! We did move into a quarter after about two months and it was such a joy. We were only there about three months when Ben was posted. This time to the reformed Central Flying School, Little Rissington, as Chief Instructor – it was a job just after his own heart. We moved into a very nice quarter but were shortly moved into another. This move was made easy for us, for we had the help of a number of German POWs who carried things from one house to the other in the snow. We had a very severe winter, Little Rissington was snowed up for six weeks and we had some supplies dropped by air. It was a lovely station though, and we got to love the Cotswolds.

Mark III, or the postscript, arrived while we were at Little Rissington, or was actually born in Cheltenham, and was in the shape of a bonny, bouncing baby girl whom we named Pipyn. She too has been the most wonderful and precious daughter to me. Peter adored her from the start and it was sweet to see him, when he came home from his prep school in the holidays, feeding her with a bottle and helping with the bathing! – not a bit embarrassed. However, Penny would only just tolerate her sister. I suppose it is always most difficult being the middle child, for it is always a case of "leave him alone, he is too old for you" or "give it to her, she is only a baby". Anyway, as the years have passed Pipyn and Penny have become firm friends and the six years between them seem to have shortened. It was while we were in this quarter that we kept hens. We also had a very young and innocent looking batman. One day I came in from the hen house and said, "Roberts, we have a broody hen. We must get some eggs and put them under her." Whereupon Peter turned to Roberts and very solemnly said, "Roberts, do you know Mummy has been broody *three* times?" – complete collapse of the batman!

I was still very unwell from time to time, but made some wonderful friends, among them a war widow who was in the WRAF. When I had to go to Cheltenham to see the doctor, I used to come home and find supper all ready in the bottom of the Aga and the fire lit etc. It was not until a long time later that I learnt that she had lost her husband and two sons during the War and had herself had a broken back! How petty my ailments seemed. It is amazing how one can always find someone who is much worse off than oneself if one looks around.

The days flew by at Little Rissington and when it was time to be posted, Ben applied for Singapore, but we were sent to Scotland – it began with an 'S' anyway! We were to go to Pitreavie Castle and he was to be Wing Commander Org, which didn't please him after his lovely flying job! However, he enjoyed it in the end. We decided to go to Scotland by car, a wee Morris Eight which we had had a trailer made for. We stuffed it with prams, cots, guns and all our precious bits and pieces, and set off one early morning with the two girls, Peter being at school. The first night we slept in Preston – and only got there by sheer luck! Our lights had failed some miles before we reached that town and, if it hadn't been for a kind lorry driver who drove slowly in front of us and allowed us to share his lights, we would have had to stop at the side of the road for hours – with two restless children, that wouldn't have been any fun!

The next morning we set off optimistically for Carlisle and all went well until we got to Kendal, when the trailer tow bar broke – but practically outside a blacksmith's shop! We had been wondering all along whether or not our wee car 'Horace' would get us all up Shap Fell, and now this happened. Ben went inside to see the blacksmith who said he couldn't have it ready for several hours, but suggested that it might be an idea to find a lorry driver who could take the trailer over Shap Fell for us seeing that we had two small children and wanted to get to Carlisle before dark. So we went around to the car park and there found a most charming man who said he had an empty lorry and certainly would help. He said he would load the trailer when it was ready and then meet Ben in the main square in Carlisle at about 6.30pm. We just left everything in the trailer as it was, took no names and addresses, and set off. The Almighty had played the game for us again as the car would never have pulled the trailer up the hill. Things couldn't have worked out better as the lorry driver delivered the goods on time and was delighted with his ten shilling tip.

On to Aberdour the next day, where we stayed for a week at *the* Hotel – the best food in Scotland it was said, and rightly so I think. But all the time we were frantically looking for a house for we couldn't afford to stay there a day longer than the week! Eventually Ben found a house, he always did somehow, even when everyone else said it was quite impossible. This time it really was a Hobson's choice, but we thought we would try it. Ironically the house was called 'Sunnyside' and was minute, had gas from a shilling-in-the-slot meter, and had a bath in the kitchen. This latter feature divided the cooker from the coal hole, so that one could cook the dinner and fill the coal scuttle while bathing! The absence of crockery was remarkable. I think we had two cups, odd plates and a tea pot without a lid. Furnished it was called, and for only three and a half guineas a week! We stayed there for about two months, during which time both the girls had chickenpox very badly and Ben managed to slip a disc while playing football for the Officers against the Sergeants. He did so very badly too, slip the disc I mean, and was in agony for days. I had to even help him dress and he had to roll himself slowly out of bed. Through pure determination though he cured himself, although there are times still when his back gives him trouble, it's not surprising really when one thinks of the number of jolts it has had one way and another.

Eventually we couldn't bear picnicking any longer and asked if we might buy some Woolworth's china to supplement the meagre issue, but we had a curt letter saying that as we were displeased, please accept a months notice! Gladly we did so, and moved into a boarding house called 'Red House' which could only have us for a couple of months before the summer season started, for they took no 'regulars'. During this brief interlude though, we managed to find yet another house, this time a huge typical Scottish mansion called 'White Hall'! It was dark and dreary and festooned with spiders' webs. In fact, in the corners of the bedrooms they had nests as big as birds nests and the ceilings were so high it was impossible to reach them with an ordinary broom. We had a couple of rooms upstairs and a kitchen downstairs. The man of the house explained that his wife wasn't 'very well', and we were to discover later that the poor thing was mental. She used to roam the house in a nightie looking, as she would say, for 'wee monsters'. One day she signed a paper to say she would enter a hospital for voluntary treatment and Ben drove her there! The owner was a scream too, for he always put on a hat and coat to answer the telephone! In lots of ways though we were very happy there, but it was in this house that I hurt my back too. One evening after putting the girls to bed, I sat in a chair and just got stuck and couldn't move. I had to sit there until about 11.00pm when Ben came back from duty. All this in 1951.

One evening we decided as a great treat to take Penny to the cinema. It was some children's film I remember, and before it was screened a news reel was shown of a zoo. She clutched my hand and whispered, "Are those real lions?" "Yes, darling," I replied. Whereupon she stood up and said, "Well I'm getting out of here!" We persuaded her to stay though. We also had a charming nanny for Pipyn while we were here, Elizabeth by name, and she was wonderful to her, and to me. They had a large black retriever at their home and Pipyn used to love riding on it.

After a few months we were given a quarter at Pitreavie Castle, a Seco hut or prefab. It had at one time been the station armoury and we re-christened it 'Chez Haggis' – it really was such fun. Although tiny, we had a terrific squeeze to get us all in plus Granny who had came over to stay, for she was practically dying of starvation in Ireland. She had been living by herself and not bothering to cook.

Ben and I had a lovely holiday while we were in Scotland. We managed to park the girls, jump into the car and make our way up north, stopping where we wished. We took a picnic lunch every day, slept in wee cottage bed and breakfasts' and poached most of the rivers! We went right to a place called Betty Hill on the north coast via the Shin Falls, where we watched the salmon leaping – and we were watched in turn by the keeper! Then it was down the east coast via Aberdeen, where the pedestrians are most conscious of their rights, they never give way to a motorist and really believe they own the roads.

Soon the day came to leave Scotland, and Ben was posted to the Joint Services Staff College at Latimer. This meant having to find somewhere for me and the children once more, and we decided to return to Camberley in the meantime and look for something from there. We motored, leaving Pitreavie in a great flourish, but when we got to Edinburgh discovered that we had left my fur coat hanging behind the bedroom door. A telephone call organised for it to be left at the RAF Club by the next officer to visit London.

While staying at the Prior's Kitchen, we met another guest who was to become one of my greatest friends, Paddy. She was tired of this existence and when we found a cottage, said she would come and be a paying guest with me while Ben was at Latimer. As soon as we moved in, I retired to bed with dry pleurisy and she had to do all the chores when she got back from work. It was enough to put most people off, but she was really wonderful. I was in bed all day of course, and Pipyn, who was about two and a half, was free to roam as she would and was always bringing me in bunches of dandelions etc. One day she came in with a gorgeous bunch of real flowers when I said, "Where did you get them from darling?" She quite honestly replied, "In the lady's garden. She was out!" At the weekend Ben took her around to apologise, but luckily the owner was very sweet and laughed the whole thing off. Near the cottage were two electric rail lines, gated of course, but to our horror one day we found Pipyn, complete with tricycle, in the field on the other side of the railway lines from our house. She had crossed through the gates on her own and it was a miracle she wasn't killed, for the trains are every few minutes. Also, if she had wheeled her trike off the wooden path she would have been electrocuted.

Both the girls had measles here too, and developed them while Paddy was baby sitting for the weekend, at which time we had gone up to London to do the Festival! Poor Paddy, her friendship had been sorely tried. Later we moved into another house at Crowthorne, a lovely house, and our three months there went all too quickly. Off again, this time to Wellesbourne Mountford near Stratford-upon-Avon, where Ben was to be the commanding officer, and a group captain – it was 1952.

The wee house we managed to get was called 'Four Chimneys' and was in the village of Tiddington. It really was a grim house, so badly furnished and the cooking arrangements so poor. It could have been made very nice, but people just expected the RAF to make do, while charging exorbitant rents. It was while we were in this house that we heard of the death of King George VI. We all felt as if we had lost a very personal friend. He was indeed a great man.

A couple of months and we up sticks again, this time to the top floor of an old country house at Loxley. This had once been the servants quarters, but now it was the CO's residence! How times have changed! The windows were all so high one couldn't see out of them, but we were happy there and it was much nearer camp. More minor tragedies: for here I broke my achilles tendon one day, playing tennis; and then Pipyn developed mumps, which I promptly caught and couldn't go down to see Peter or Penny who were both in boarding school in Camberley. We also had some American cousins to stay while we were in this house and they were fascinated with the 'Cute little old English home'. I am sure in their hearts they must have thought how archaic it all was.

It was here too that we had another young batman and I can remember telling him that when the Air Marshal Sir Charles Steele came to tea, he was to open the front door, take his hat etc. After listening to me for a bit he said, "Madam, when Lord Steele…" "No, not Lord Steele, Sir Charles Steele…," I replied. Whereupon he gave a shrug of his shoulders and said, "Same meat, different gravy." In desperation I gave him the afternoon off!

Eventually we moved onto the camp into a Nissen hut type of house, designated to be the CO's quarters. Although it had everything possible against it, we loved that house and made it a real home. Its front was on the main road and its back garden practically in the MT (mechanical transport) section but all the same, it had something. We loved our time here at Wellesbourne and apart from the fun we had on the station, the local population was so friendly. The countryside was beautiful too, and of course there was the theatre. Ben and I both had a horror of Shakespeare from our school days and we thought we would never be converted. In sheer desperation, we decided we must creep off and see some of the plays, for we felt so out of the conversation at parties and so ashamed when we could not voice an opinion. We did go, and became absolute fans – wouldn't miss a production if we could help it.

~ Chapter Five ~

THE MIDDLE EAST

"News," said Ben one day as he rushed in, "we have been posted." It was a great thrill to hear that we were going to Habbaniya in Iraq. He was to be Senior Air Staff Officer, Iraq. We were to go in four months time and I was to be able to travel with him and take the two girls. Peter had to stay behind as he was just spending his last term at prep school and going on to Rossall. I had some dreadful heart rending and sometimes, in the middle of the night, I used to wake up and say to myself, "It's no use, I can't leave him," and then in the pale light of dawn I would realise that I wasn't the only mother that had been called upon to leave her child. What of those mothers during the War who had their children forcibly taken from them, never to be seen again. Surely I could master enough pluck to do this thing. And with the help of the Almighty I did. I shall never forget though the whiteness of Peter's face when he left me – he never cried, always just went white. I knew the terrible blankness he felt inside him.

Anyway all that was still four months away and we had endless things to do before we finally left Wellesbourne. And it wasn't helped either by the fact that within a few days after receiving the news of our posting, the Air Ministry told us that Ben would have to go alone and we could follow a few weeks afterwards. Fair enough, but even later they phoned to say that I couldn't go in the foreseeable future. Panics, for we had no home. It meant looking for somewhere to live, unpacking all the things that we had put jointly in a trunk etc and of course, all our inoculations were to no avail. However, another phone call and the voice at the end said, "When could your wife and children be ready to go?" "Now," said Ben. The man at the other end didn't believe him and it took several minutes for Ben to be able to persuade him that he really meant '*now*', for hadn't we been packed and jabbed weeks ago? "Right," he said, "you may all travel together." Wonderful, but I am sure many of our friends found it hard to believe how any institution could chop and change so!

Peter left to stay with our friends, the McAulays, who also took our Morris Eight and the scottie, Haggisse. Peter was to stay with them for a few days before going to Rossall and it was extra hard for him to go there before the *first* term on his own. The girls spent our final night at Wellesbourne with some friends in the village and we collected them after breakfast and went to Leamington to catch our train for London where we were to spend the night at an RAF transit camp at Hendon. I can see Pipyn to this day settling down in the corner and saying loud and clear, "At last I am seeing the world." Out of the mouths of babes and sucklings… this was October 1953.

We had lunch at the Euston Hotel with Granny and then by bus to Hendon, where we were herded together with the other passengers who were also going to Hab. In fact we discovered that Ben was to be the only man amongst forty women and children! It was early to bed and then up at 4.30am, to be faced with the inevitable eggs and beans, and then a long drive to Stanstead in Essex for a 9.30am take-off – or so it should have been. The children and I were full of pills to prevent air sickness and we felt fine while sitting on the ground, which we did until midday, then we clambered into an old York which somehow lumbered into the air. Ben had spent the whole of the previous evening finding maps of our route and folding them correctly. However, when he turned around to show me where we were, he found that I had a bright green face and wasn't in the least interested in the fact that I was being sick above the Eiffel Tower – the same with the children. What a journey he had, almost everyone in that aircraft was sick and he spent the time helping the air hostess with paper bags. It was a brief landing at Malta, then on into the night, and eventually to be in Cyprus at 2.30am. We were up again at 7.00am and on over the desert to Habbaniya. I'll never forget my first sight of the desert, it wasn't flat, soft and sandy as I had imagined, but hard, bumpy and a dull red. There were miles and miles of it, and I wondered so much what would happen if we had had to land on it. All the same, it was fascinating and it was a fascination none of us were ever to lose.

Near Habbaniya we saw the Euphrates and then the lake, fifty miles in circumference, and then the camp which was a perfect looking oasis, which it proved to be too. As we stepped out of the aircraft it was like stepping into an oven, but it was only 108°F. We were to learn that in July and August the temperature rose to 120°F in the shade. To transit camp again – and again eggs and beans! We couldn't face them and at last were shown our rooms: cool, low with fans, and mosquito netting. Our luggage arrived in due course, and we were told that we would have to spend seven weeks in transit for there was no house for us – the Air Ministry had made a mistake! I was so thankful they didn't discover it in time, and would willingly have camped under a palm tree to avoid being left behind in England.

Everyone was so kind and life at first was a little strange, although the whole countryside reminded me so much of places of my youth, Mafeking in particular. Ben was given a sandy coloured staff car and a wonderful Assyrian driver called Charlie, who was to become my firm friend in the months to come. The cars were all left hand drive and of course, one drove on the right side of the road. Habbaniya was a camp above all camps in spite of being in the middle of the desert: gorgeous swimming pools; churches of all denominations; cinema; and every known sport almost, riding, sailing, tennis, golf (rather rugged), cricket, archery, football, squash and of course the endless swimming. The water in the baths was just as I liked it, never below 76°F and often at about midnight, almost 82°F in spite of constant spraying to try and keep it cool. There was also the most lovely park called Command Gardens where almost everything was grown and in the spring, the roses and sweet peas defied description. There were hedges of the latter, while common things like zinnias grew to about nine feet tall!

The first present that Charlie produced for us was a mongoose. Ricky we called him, but he escaped soon after we moved into a house and lived in a hole in the garden. I remember asking Charlie to buy me a few dates and gave him fifty fils, the equivalent of a shilling. He came back with a complete bunch, which we hung outside the door and to which every passer-by helped themselves. Our neighbours in transit were a family who had three little boys, the middle one of which Pipyn didn't like at all. He used to tease her endlessly but she got her own back by pushing him into the baths, fully clothed. We didn't hear about it for a long time, and apparently his mother was as amused as we were. Both the girls soon learned to swim, in fact it was amazing to see small children swimming before they could walk. Everyone spent as much time as possible in the baths and it was a wonderful experience for all the children.

We had only been at Hab about two days when the AOC commanded our presence at dinner. My heart sank, for his parties were notorious for their late hours and I was still feeling unwell after the journey. However, there was nothing else we could do but go. I lasted out until about 10.30pm when I thought popularity or no popularity, I must go home to bed. Whereupon I got up and, before I could make a good night speech, the AOC had leaped forward, offered his hand and practically shown us the door. There was a horrified look on all the other faces, for their owners had thought they were settling down to a nice long night of drinking, but of course they had more or less to follow suit and leave, for I was the senior lady.

The next morning Ben went in to thank him for the party expecting to get a rocket for leaving so early, but the AOC asked him to give me a message. "Tell your wife," he said, "that she may come to Air House whenever she likes as long as she always leaves at 10.30." Apparently he was fed up with people sitting on ad infinitum. In fact he used to ask us to particularly difficult dinners so that we would leave early and take the others with us. He used to give me a wink when he had had enough, and off we set!

After about five weeks we moved into a charming little bungalow in Palm Grove, or Millionaires Row and Snobs Alley as it was jokingly called. Our house was opposite to the baths and we could just walk down the garden path in our swimming costumes. However, it was in the middle of the row and didn't have much privacy so later on, when we got the chance, we moved to another similar house at the end of the row. There we could sleep out on the lawns during the summer months without being seen by passers-by, for we had a huge lawn on which we had grown a three sided hedge. This was a tremendously quick growing hedge, about a foot a week it grew, and we had a complete hide in about a month. The fourth side to the square was formed by the house, and it was gorgeous sleeping out and gazing at the stars. They seemed so near somehow and the moon almost kept us awake at times it was so bright. It never rained in the summer months, but the whole camp was flooded in sections with Euphrates water, during the nights we would wake about every ten days and find our beds standing in water. If we had left our slippers on the lawn instead of on the end of the bed, they would be afloat. In this way the whole place was kept wonderfully green. There were some wonderful old Arab men called water wallahs who used to roam the camp putting in bungs or taking them out as the case might be. I have always thought it must be about the most perfect of occupations!

Thieving is the national sport of the Arabs, and we succeeded in losing two bicycles and a blanket off the bed while we were at Hab. Before a prospective father-in-law will give his consent to his daughters marriage, he is quite likely to test the worthiness of her future husband by saying, "You can marry Fatima if you bring me the blanket off the Group Captain's bed." Whereupon the ambitious youth would proceed to pinch it while the officer was asleep – and usually managed it without detection. Arab bearers also had a wonderful habit of 'borrowing' and when one went out to dinner, it was quite common to find that one was using one's own glasses because probably the host's bearer thought yours to be slightly superior to his memsahib's! Alternatively, you would be amazed to find your meat course at your own dinner party appearing on someone else's plates. We had great trouble persuading our bearer that our silver candelabra were nice. He used to grumble every time we had them on the table and said it looked like church. In fact he would put them on the table for breakfast, and I had to insist that we only had them for dinner. He also had a wonderful imagination, for I had shown him how to decorate a chocolate mousse with angelica and cherries etc. One day they appeared with some unusual decorations which I couldn't fathom at all. It wasn't until I asked him, that I found he had used grated carrot because the NAAFI hadn't sent the proper things – very nice it was.

Abid was a wonderful character. He had his off days when he was very sulky and the 'Wind was in the East' we used to say when one just avoided the kitchen. These days were very few and far between though, and mostly he used to sing in that peculiar gippy tummy music that only the Arabs can use. When that ceased, we knew that tiffin was ready and he had fallen asleep on the kitchen table awaiting our call. He was very punctual with our early morning tea at 5.30am, and was never late. When I asked him how he managed it and if he had an alarm clock he said, "No, memsahib, I have an alarm *cock*." It appeared that our feathered friend was tied underneath his bed and got him up in good time every morning.

One morning however he was late, but arrived in due course with his head swathed in bandages. We discovered that someone had waylaid him and practically split his skull in two. He had had a tremendous amount of stitches, but had come to work all the same – most Europeans would have died. He said he had rather a headache so I sent him home with a couple of codeine. He arrived the next morning 'mended' or so he said, but for ages he had to wear a bandage! – quite incredible.

We hadn't been long at Hab before we were asked to our first cuzi. We had heard about these Arab feasts and how the honoured guest was given the sheep's eye as a token of respect and had to swallow it there and then. However, that didn't worry us, for we knew we were only small fry, but the thought of the vague possibility wasn't very pleasant. We set out at about 7.00pm for the nearby village, Ramadi, and then turned off into the desert to a very nice little house. It was winter time, so we were to be entertained inside. The room into which we were shown was furnished with sofas and chairs all lining the walls, and a centre table. Our interpreter, who was a British army officer, made the introductions. Our host was a local sheik who had gathered various friends to meet us, all in their long flowing robes and white head-dresses with a cord wound around the head to keep the kaffiyeh in place. We sat down and were asked what we would like to drink. Those who chose alcohol were presented with a bottle of their choice apiece, and the rest of us were expected to drink gallons of Coca Cola or similar. We had been warned not to ask for water for of course, it wouldn't have been boiled and was so scarce in those parts that it would probably have been put to several uses before it reached the dinner table! We sat, drank and ate nuts for three hours. The conversation didn't flow because none of us could speak Arabic apart from the Major, and our hosts only knew a few words of English, but nobody seemed to mind. The Arabs had the most wonderful way of making themselves at ease by drawing their feet up on to the sofa and sitting on them, while we were all painfully British and correct and sat as Queen Victoria would have wished us to do!

One of the 'snacks' that was passed around was some gorgeous looking cos lettuce, the biggest I have ever seen. As I took a piece, I saw our interpreter friend shaking his head violently from behind my host – too late, I had taken it. However, necessity is the mother of invention, so somehow when nobody was looking I hope, I secreted it under my fur cape which I had on my lap, and then later placed it into my bag. Going home I showed it to the Major who was somewhat appalled. However, the others who had eaten theirs, suffered for the next three days with the most awful tummy trouble. Oh yes, the lettuce had been washed, they knew the stupid British liked that, but of course it was washed in some of that unmentionable water!

Eventually we were ushered into a meal, a table spread with a huge mound of rice on which was practically a whole sheep. We helped ourselves with our hands, and ate with them too. I must confess I always rather enjoyed this, it must be a throw back to my caveman days! It did take a little time getting used to having a huge chunk of meat placed on one's plate by a large hairy hand and being expected to eat about twice one's normal capacity. Ben espied a gorgeous looking dish of trifle, he thought, for we didn't realise then that sweets were never on the menu. It was white, with cream(?) and had lovely strips of angelica(?). Oh well, he took a huge helping, and then I will never forget the look on his face when he took the first mouthful. It was a dish of sour goats milk and garlic! Poor Ben, he loathes garlic, but being a brave officer, he finished it – and paid for it for almost a week. We had both had our first lessons in discretion that evening.

Having stuffed ourselves full, we up and went. There was no sitting about afterwards, the object of the evening had been accomplished and we drove back to camp in our various desert coloured cars after a handshake all round. Our host's other friends sped across the desert in large, brightly coloured American cars to their various houses or tents. Somehow it always seemed wrong to me to see an Arab with a flowing head-dress speeding by in a huge car. It would have been so much nicer to have seen him set off on a camel.

We attended lots of these cuzis and I always enjoyed them, especially those out in the open and one in particular we went to across the Euphrates, where we sat in a small encampment. It was here that the sheik's guards patrolled around us with rifles at the ready, it really seemed so romantic and quite out of Beau Geste! We also went to one very set-up 'do' given by the Muttaserrif, or Mayor, of Ramadi, and this was a sit down dinner. We saw with horror that there were seven sets of 'eating irons' in each place, so we ate a little of everything and were sitting back replete, when the bearer put another five sets in front of each person. We couldn't believe our eyes and felt sure too that our skins would never make the grade and would simply have to burst. Then came the curry and after that four various other courses. In the end we had had twelve dishes! Several of our Iraqi friends even had second helpings, but I know none of us could face much food for the next two or three days. The Mayor was a wonderful character and took us to a night club in Baghdad once, where we saw the most revolting(?) tummy wobbler dancers. I often wonder what happened to him, and many others, during the Revolt of 1958.

In summer, work started at 6.00am on the camp and finished at 1.00pm with a break for breakfast in between, then we had the afternoon to sleep or do as we wished. Most afternoons Ben sailed and I sat in the lake, literally, and supplied him and his crew with pints and pints of liquid when they came in. Our intake of water was quite amazing, and it was nothing to down three pints without stopping. In fact my standing order at the NAAFI was seven dozen Coca Colas a week, and that didn't count all the odd drinks we had out, water, tea, coffee and squash etc. Pipyn used to sail with Ben, and in fact won the Ladies Race at one regatta – at the age of seven! Conversely, his mother also sailed at Hab, aged seventy-five, and won a race too! I am the only landlubber in our family and when Peter flew out for the summer holidays, he had great fun sailing too. To this day he bears two scars across his chest that he got on the side of the boat when trying to save Ben's watch from falling into the water. We used to have moonlight sails and moonlight picnics too and, with the temperature at about 90°F at midnight, these were very pleasant.

One day I was asked to do a Desert Island Disc programme on the local broadcasting service. This I did and enjoyed it very much. Then the officer in charge asked me if I would consider becoming an Aunt on Children's Hour – Yes, I would! He said I would have to have a test just to make the thing correct, and I read a story which was recorded and then played back to a panel of five, consisting of four airmen and himself. "Well, what do you think Corporal?" he asked one of them. "Quite good," said the corporal, "but *terribly* BBC!" – I got the job. This eventually led to more and more broadcasting until one day I became the Chief Announcer. I must say it was all the greatest fun and an experience I wouldn't have missed for anything. It wasn't quite as simple perhaps as it sounds, for being an announcer on the forces system entailed being a jack of all trades. It was our job to switch on all the mechanism which set things in motion if one was first on at 6.00am and switching them off in the evening after the last shift. This was really petrifying as there seemed to be a tremendous amount of knobs and if they weren't switched in the correct order, one was likely to blow the whole thing up.

Hab was about sixty miles from Baghdad and there was a road of sorts, but most cars used the hard desert. When flying over this part, the dust from the cars looked exactly like the wake a ship makes when steaming at full speed. One arrived in Baghdad covered in dust, hot and sticky but it was all worth it. Baghdad itself is the most wonderful place, I think. Wonderful if one doesn't mind smells and flies, for both these abound in vast and varying quantities. The traffic goes at two speeds, flat out or stop, with continuous blowing of horns such as I am convinced is never heard anywhere else. The pavements are given over to camels or mules while pedestrians take their luck on the crowded streets. The whole city is full of little alley ways known as suqs, which are fascinating to the extreme – copper suqs, gold suqs, silver suqs, material suqs etc. I am quite certain that I would never ever have got tired of visiting Baggers, as we used to call it.

The children loved their visits there too, and on one occasion we all went on a conducted tour to Babylon. Our guide was a Mr Lampard who was very knowledgeable and had been with the YMCA in Baghdad for about thirty years. He was a tremendous talker, but even he was beaten by Pipyn who commandeered him and talked and asked questions the entire time! It was a wonderful place to have seen, some of the bricks are still perfect after five thousand years and many motifs can still be seen on the walls. The one thing that rather spoilt it for us was that when we got there a crowd of Iraqi students were playing a gramophone with Rock an' Roll, or the equivalent, records in the middle of the great dining hall! We left them and wandered around the ruins, our imagination running riot and stimulated by a little scroll which Mr Lampard picked up and gave Pipyn as a souvenir – she still has it. We then went on to the Tower of Babel and climbed as high as we could, having a good view of the surrounding desert. How wonderful it must have all been in its day. I wonder how many bricks of our cathedrals will be perfect in the year 7000? When we got back to the city we went around the museum, a thing which Pipyn insisted on doing whenever we came to town, regardless of the temperature. I must say it was a place of unending interest and one thing that impressed us almost more than most, was a golden dagger which the curator struck hard into a piece of teak – these days no one knows how to temper gold.

One day Ben's job necessitated that he should do an inspection of some of the places in northern Iraq with a view to building landing grounds. We had the most wonderful trip with another group captain, a doctor, a driver (Charlie) and ourselves. We spent the first night at a place called Erbil which one can see for miles before reaching it. It looks from the distance exactly like a pork pie in the middle of the desert, for it has been built-up during the last five thousand years or so, each generation building on top of the rubble left by falling houses etc. In fact it is the oldest continuously inhabited town in the world. Alexander the Great rested here, and at one time it was a great meeting place of all the caravan routes. The new town lies at its foot and it was here that we found the rest house. This was very nice and quite adequate, although I am not really sure that the sheets had been washed since the last traveller slept in my bed! It's a funny thing, but even after sleeping in a vast number of different beds, I still get the creeps when I have to get into a new one – unless it is obviously new and very pure!

We stayed the night at Erbil and visited the old town which was supposed to be out of bounds, but only because there was no sanitation there. The next day we went on up the mountain valley to a place called Sulaimaniya. This was lovely, and the whole countryside was green and covered with little white star of bethlehem flowers and crocus etc. The streams flowed fast and it had the great appearance of Scotland. It was hard to believe that the desert was lying side by side with all this. This was to be our first meeting with Kurds and we found them a proud people, who nevertheless seemed quite amazed at a white female wandering through their market place. This I insisted on doing, for I adore these places. Poor Charlie had fits I think, and thought I was going to be knifed at any moment – he stuck closer than a shadow. We bought a sack of walnuts here for next to nothing, and two lots of honey. The honey was in a mud hive and was very nice, not unlike heather honey, when one had removed the bits of earth and straw.

On another occasion we took the road north instead of east, and went past Erbil on to Mosul. This time we spent the night at the oil station in Kirkuk, a fascinating place where the Eternal Fires of the Bible are. I walked into the middle of a circle of flames, which was supposed to bring one luck. I learnt here too that during the War they tried to cover up these flames because of course, they were such a landmark – they never succeeded in doing so. The flames are made by escaping gas from the oil below. It is a wonderful camp with a super rest house, everything is very modern and beautifully kept. There is a free taxi service for the employees and petrol is only sixpence a gallon, that being the tax imposed by the Iraqi government.

At Mosul we had breakfast with the Iraqi Air Force and then on to the King's Summer Palace at Sirsingh, which was near the one time RAF rest and leave camp at Sirarmadia. The road to these places passes Nineveh, which looks like a few mud ruins and has none of its former glory. The countryside is heavenly, Scotland all over again – so cool and refreshing. The hotel was very modern, but there were no bath plugs. Although we had a private bathroom, we had to content ourselves with showers. There was a small swimming pool which we shared with the waiters, who joined us when they had no customers! We did several motor trips from here, and one day went to a village from where one rides to Sirarmadia on mule back. Ben had a bad knee so contented himself with sketching, while Brian and Philip decided to make the ascent on mule back. As I hate riding, I decided I was going to walk some of the way accompanied of course, by the faithful Charlie.

It was very rough going: up a mountain path, past huge boulders and across little streams. It was a case of one way traffic most of the time. We met several Kurds with their pack mules and had to stand on rocks to let them pass. We got three quarters of the way up, rested and then started on the return journey. I was dying to answer the call of nature, but nothing I could suggest would persuade Charlie to leave me for a moment, and when I said I was just going to bathe my feet in a stream, he insisted on coming too and even washed them for me. So I just had to suffer until we got back to the hotel!

At the bottom of the hill we bought some Kurdish pipes of varying length. These were lovely pieces of wood covered in different silks with a small bowl at the end. The length of them varied from a few inches to about four feet. As the good mohammedan doesn't allow tobacco to come in contact with his lips, a cigarette is placed in the small bowl and enjoyed that way! The Kurds also made fascinating shoes for walking up and down the rocky paths out of old motor car tyres.

On our way back south we turned off and took a road to Rowanduz – a real feat of engineering. The road to Rowanduz is tarmac'd all the way, winds uphill and the views are too beautiful to describe. In one place one can look back and see seventeen terraces of road where we had wound our way up and up. The gorges are deep and frightening at times, and on one occasion we drove under a huge hanging rock where they had just had to blast a way for the road to pass, right through the mountainside – it was almost like a tunnel.

We stopped at one gorge and fished, Charlie and me with great success with a bent nail and some bread, while the others didn't catch a thing with all their wonderful equipment! The fish were most tantalising for one could see them lying on the bottom of the river and just refusing to take any notice of us. There were lovely waterfalls and fern and the rivers were deep and swift running, for they were being fed by melting snows. Even in midsummer there were two or three mountain tops still covered with snow – really beautiful.

As we were picnicking, a band of Kurds appeared, armed to the teeth, but Charlie (who could speak eight languages, but write and read none) came to our rescue and we had a friendly, if one sided chat. In the end, they were showing us their firearms and even let Ben shoot with one of their rifles – a great privilege as ammunition is very precious. They asked us to take their photographs, which we did, and then later sent them the required number of copies to the post office at Haji O Maraan. This was also our place of rest for the night, for there was a rest house there, and a very nicely run one too. It was a very popular place in the winter and was frequented by skiing enthusiasts. It was about three miles from the border with Persia, and the following morning we drove to the boundary and met a Persian warrant officer in charge of the fort there. He showed us around and offered us tea. While we were chatting, a Persian with a simply gorgeous carpet for sale passed by, and laid his wares on the dirty sandy road for us to see. The carpet was a gorgeous one of peacock blues and wines. We would have loved to buy it, but we had no spare money with us in spite of the price being ridiculously low – I have always regretted it!

At Haji O Maraan we were told that there had been a phone call for us from the British Embassy in Baghdad, but when we tried to phone we were told that the line was only open for two hours in the early morning. We would have to wait for the following day as the operator was off over the hills hunting and no one else understood 'the thing'. You can imagine how our thoughts ran riot that night, for we had left the children with Granny and felt one of them must at least be ill for there to have been such an important phone call for us. However, eventually we did get to sleep and Ben was on the phone as soon as possible the next day. The line was terribly bad, but we did manage to gather that all was well at home, but we had been posted to Cyprus within ten days, for the Air Headquarters Middle East Air Force was moving over there.

We were awfully sad at this news, for we loved Iraq so much that we could have stayed there forever! We knew that this was bound to happen some day as we had recently witnessed the handing over ceremony when Habbaniya was handed back to the Iraqis after the expiration of the lease, but somehow it seemed to come so suddenly. Ben always tells a lovely tale of how the camp was turned from a British base to an Arab camp within minutes, for during the actual ceremony the Union Jack was lowered at the guard room, and an Iraqi flag hoisted; the guards changed from RAF Levies to Iraqi soldiers; and all semblance of British rule was swept away by the flag being raised on a pole which was made almost secure by huge rocks at its base, so that it naturally had the lean that all Arabic flag poles have. The guards of course, knew practically no English and when we were asked the equivalent of, "Who goes there," we usually replied, "Happy Christmas," or some such nonsense and the boom was lifted immediately! Happy days – all to end so soon and so abruptly.

During our two years we were lucky enough to visit Jerusalem. The AOC wanted a Humber staff car driven up to Amman and when we got there, we were to stay with the commanding officer of the RAF base. We had known him before and were much looking forward to seeing him and his family again. Unfortunately, we decided that the trip would be too hot and tiring for Granny, so we left her at Hab and had to leave Pipyn to look after her. I have always regretted the latter, for although she was young she would have enjoyed it as much as the rest of us and probably learnt far more.

The sun coming over the desert was perfect, exactly as one sees it in the picture postcards. The day got hotter and hotter and, although the scenery was all exactly the same, it was simply fascinating. To me the odd camel skeleton always helped to conjure up so many pictures. We saw several caravans too, several hundred strong some of them, but the thing that amazed me most was to see plenty of birds. Small ones admittedly, but with no water in sight, I suppose they lived on the moisture they got from the insects they caught. We saw lots of mirages and, as the day wore on, we got more and more thirsty, but luckily had taken lots of water with us. At the various pipeline stations along the way we were able to obtain tea, at least it was always offered. We drank endless cups of the sweet lime tea without milk and praised the Arabs for their hospitality. The pipeline stations were closed, but were just being maintained in the hopes that one day they would be in operation again when the Israelis allowed the oil to flow once more to Haifa, or until another outlet to a port was found.

Several times we had to stop and turn the Humber around to allow the engine to cool in the slight breeze, for we were travelling with the wind and the sun was so hot that everything became overheated very quickly – including ourselves. I remember I had developed a bad headache and thought that all I wanted in the world was some cold water for my feet and a bowl of fruit salad! The road in places was dead straight for thirty-two miles – that was the longest stretch we measured without a bend in it.

We stopped at the extra special pumping station H4 and had a cold shower and tea and then continued onto Mafraq, a big landing stage in Jordan. Before we got there the desert changed though from brown and red sandy stretches to great piles and hillocks made up of hard, black and most inhospitable looking rock. Mafraq was in the stage of being expanded and there were still a terrific number of airmen living in tents, the whole place was to become very large and have a huge airfield. From there we drove on to Amman, and one the most pitiful sights met our eyes – endless refugees living in the most indescribable hovels and even in caves in the side of the hills. These people had all come from Israel.

We simply fell into bed that night, but it was lovely to be comparatively cool for the station was on a hill. It was lovely too to see all the lights of Amman from across a small valley. Lights that were scattered over the hills and seemed to stretch for a long way and which seemed so hospitable after the long stretch of uninhabited desert.

The following morning we went into Amman and visited the various suqs buying the odd souvenir, notably some Arab Legion head-dresses. We were also shown the King's palaces and altogether thought it was a lovely spot. After lunch our host took us to a place called Jerash, a couple of hours drive away, across hills and with a very windy road. This didn't please poor Penny a bit, for she was inclined to be nervous and car sick if the road was too full of bends. We picnicked en route and when we got to the ruins, we could hardly believe our eyes – they were simply beautiful. Huge columns were still standing, terraces with fountains and seats were still in reasonable repair. The whole place had once been a Roman rest and leave centre and was built on the same lines as many other Roman bases. The whole place was most fascinating and I could have spent days wandering around instead of the few hours we had. Excavations were still going on and I hope one day we shall pay another visit, and this time have Pipyn with us. I thought it was one of the most impressive places I had ever seen.

The following day we hired a car and went to Jerusalem. The car was a huge American one, with the accelerator set at about forty miles per hour so that when the driver took his foot off, we cruised at that speed. I found it somewhat alarming on the very tortuous road, especially as the more severe the corner, the faster it went – honestly! We couldn't persuade Penny to come with us unfortunately, as her trip the previous day had put her off, after hearing that the road to the Holy City was even worse.

We did arrive there in one piece and it was wonderful to travel through the land where our Lord had trod, and down a road that was probably used by the Good Samaritan. It all seemed so unchanged somehow, although how was I to know? The desert has remained the same for thousands of years, and it didn't take much imagination to picture robbers swooping down from the hills. We passed several hamlets too where the Inn of the Bible story could so easily have been placed. Our first sight of Jerusalem was just as we had pictured it from many old sketches. Of course we were only to be able to visit half of the city, for a boundary had been drawn right through the middle of it. This boundary was manned by armed guards all day and night, and there were many barbed wire entanglements.

We had lunch at our hotel and then set off on our sightseeing. Although it was simply wonderful to have been able to have gone to Jerusalem, it is somehow disappointing. The whole place has been so commercialised, and as one enters the various holy spots one is besieged by priests of all denominations trying to sell postcards and souvenirs. There is so little peace and quiet and somehow it all seemed so overcrowded. We visited the different Stations of the Cross, the Wailing Wall and the Mosque of Omar. I am ashamed to say that this mosque to me, was one of the most beautiful places. It was cool, quiet, with carpets said to be at least three hundred years old, and in the centre a rock bearing the footprint of Mohammed from where he is said to have been received up in heaven. The mosque is on the site of the Old Temple where our Lord turned out the money changers etc.

We then went to see two places where our Lord was said to have been buried, but the one we thought and felt the most likely was just outside the old city wall. It was called the Garden Tomb and here in the peace of a lovely garden, we found a hole in the rock with a stone ledge for the body, and outside was a huge wheel of granite which ran along a groove to close the door. This place was just beyond a hill which General Gordon thought must have been the original Golgotha or Place of the Skull. He noticed from his hotel window how much the hillside just outside the city gates resembled a human skull, and the site of the Garden Tomb was just a little further up the road out of the city.

The next day we went to the Garden of Gethsemane. This was lovely and so calm and so as one imagined a place would be where our Lord would choose to pray. The old olive trees were crooked and gnarled and one felt they had been standing there at the time. Next to the garden is a lovely church: simple, beautiful and most restful; and called the Church of the Nations. Here one could think, whereas in the various shrines there seemed to be such overcrowding and bustle and noise.

We then went on to Bethlehem and our guide showed us the field in which the shepherds were supposed to have seen the angels. The Church of the Nativity was surrounded with scaffolding. Here again one got the feeling of never being left alone, although it was very beautiful. We loved being able to see all those wonderful places and I hope you don't think I am being unkind in all that I have said. Of course it must have been so different in our Lord's day, but it was marvellous indeed to think we had stood on *the* spot where he had trod.

Our visit was brief, but we were still to visit Jericho and the Dead Sea on our return to Amman. Jericho is in the middle of a flat, hot plain and we saw no sign of the walls as our driver seemed to be in such a hurry – we didn't have time to explore! We did go down to the Dead Sea, and how terribly hot and sticky it was. The men bathed and of course the sea is so salty, it is impossible to sink. I sat and watched them and drank the inevitable Coca Cola.

It was all over far too quickly and soon we were on our way from Amman back to Habbaniya. We decided to leave at about 3.00pm and drive to H4 where we would have some sleep until about 9.00pm. Then we would continue through the night the rest of the way, to avoid the great heat. This we did and the sunset was wonderful, but I am not sure which I preferred as it was so hard keeping awake. Although I was not driving, I felt it unfair to try and sleep. During the night we stopped several times for drinks etc and had to call at a customs clearing station which we reached at 3.30am. We also had to report to the immigration people at Ramadi which we reached at about 5.00am, but as we couldn't make anyone hear, we drove on and, as far as I know, we are still in Jordan! We reached Hab at sunrise, and in many ways it was lovely to be home. We slept all day and Granny and Pipyn had to wait until later in the evening before hearing all about our trip. Granny was well, but Pipyn had had prickly heat for the first time ever.

There is so much I haven't told about Habbaniya: how the apricots blossomed and were a wonderful sight; how we lived on their fruits for days, mishmash it was called; and how the chickens we had for dinner were tied to the kitchen table and then executed about an hour before we ate them, a horrible thought and one I never could really get used to. I haven't mentioned the animals we had too, and one in particular a dachshund called Rusty who was the greatest little sport and who stole all our hearts. He used to chase the jackals which roamed the camp and one day got caught in barbed wire. Ben had to get the duty MO to extract him and, although the doctor fought hard to save him and even had him in a spare cubby-hole up at the hospital, he died after choking from too much anaesthetic. Yes, the hospital, which was almost second home to us all, and it was a joke that there was almost always a Boult on the inventory. Granny started us off by going into hospital the day she arrived with pleurisy which she thought was lumbago! The doctors and staff undoubtedly saved her life. Then Pipyn developed jaundice, followed shortly by me and then by Penny who also had scarlet fever! Pipyn was in hospital nine weeks (I was in for seven) and was such a good little patient; she was so brave about having the beastly blood tests and everyone was full of admiration for her. She looked like a real yellow Chinese child with bright blue eyes!

Eventually we all got home and recovered, but Pipyn was soon back with tonsillitis and glandular fever, and then I was admitted with a poisoned thumb which would not heal in spite of the nail being taken off. I remember so well how it all 'blew up' just when Ben went off to Turkey. Charlie, the faithful Charlie, took me to hospital and his wife Maria, also a wonderful character, visited me. She was small comfort, for she just sat beside my bed and wept the whole time. I don't know whether she was sad to see me in hospital or it was pure relief at the thought I was recovering! She was a wonderful dressmaker and equipped me for my whole stay at Hab.

Shortly after we had all come out of hospital, we decided that we must take a trip to Baghdad and get the girls' pigtails cut off. There was then no ladies hairdresser on the camp, and I used to have mine cut alternatively by Ben or the Arab barber, who used to cut Ben's at the same time on our veranda. We went to the recommended barber in Baggers and he cut Poo's hair quite nicely. When it got to Pip's turn I said, "The same, but a little shorter." He spoke no English but nodded his head and proceeded to give her a *crew* cut. Horrors – I didn't know how to face Ben! She loved it however, and of course it was wonderful for swimming. The novelty soon wore off and we proceeded to grow it again – inconsistent women!

The day dawned when we had to take off for Nicosia. It was a very sad day too, although everyone made our parting as nice as they possibly could.

We had real VIP treatment, an escort of two Venoms from 6 Squadron which was most thrilling and almost a little frightening as they seemed to come so close. We had a Pembroke almost to ourselves with a lot of seats removed so that we could stretch our legs and, although I hated flying, I almost enjoyed this trip! We saw Mount Ararat in the distance and the hills of the Lebanon. In almost no time at all, four hours in fact, we reached Nicosia.

We had been looking forward to Cyprus immensely as so many people came to Hab with such glowing reports, but for the first few weeks we simply hated it. I think it was the complete contrast of not knowing anyone, being just lonely and having Ben away all day. We stayed at a hotel in Kyrenia and found it so hot. Not nearly as hot as Hab as far as temperature went, but so sticky. The sea was beautiful though, warm and clear and we soon went shoofty-scoping. We hired a car some Sundays and went for lovely drives too, but all the same, it never held such a warm place in our hearts as did Iraq. I remember receiving a huge watermelon from Charlie with 'Mrs Boult, Cyprus' carved on the side! Poor, faithful Charlie, he didn't realise of course that melons were plentiful in Cyprus. Eventually we were allocated a quarter in Nicosia, one which had just been completed. However, when the day dawned for us to move I had tonsillitis, but nothing would put me off moving out of that hotel! I remember feeling so ill too and having penicillin injections by the district nurse, or SAAFA Sister actually, to the accompaniment of the road being electrically drilled outside my window and the plumber knocking hell out of the bathroom wall to insert a towel rail!

EOKA troubles were on of course, and in some ways it was most exciting. Servants were difficult, but we did manage to get a Greek girl for a while, but one day she just "didn't come anymore" so we had to do everything. Ben went about armed and when we went shopping in Nicosia on certain mornings of the week, we went under escort. It was a creepy feeling somehow walking down 'murder mile' and just wondering… We did get caught in two riots: one, a turkish one while I was having my hair done in a Greek shop (the result was havoc!); and the other, Penny and I actually were in the middle of, and were very frightened too. This riot was outside the post office, opposite the law courts and was caused by the mob not agreeing with the death penalty passed on an EOKA youth found guilty of the murder of a civilian. We fought our way back to the taxi as the driver had refused to go nearer than a couple of side streets away – I suppose he was very wise. We were much relieved to get back to camp, somehow the crowds seemed to make such a horrible moaning noise with their chanting. Whenever we went out to dinner in RAF quarters there was always a pile of arms left on the hall table – guarded of course!

The winter came, and with it Peter's school holidays and a visit from him; his second, for he had managed to get out in the summer too. He was bitterly disappointed that it wasn't to be Hab that he was visiting again. Penny did go back to Hab for a visit, but somehow going back is never quite the same. In some ways it is such a pity to try and pick up something one has dropped with beautiful memories. All the same, I think it would be worth risking!

We went up to Mount Olympus several times. It is really beautiful there and of course in the winter, there is lots of skiing. We didn't get a chance though, for in January we were posted home for Ben to command Chivenor in Devon, or so we were told the previous October. We then heard three days before we actually left Cyprus, that we were to go to South Cerney in Gloucestershire! This was very upsetting, as we had made all our plans for Devon, schools etc, and we had been to the CFS before. Also Ben felt that it was not a good thing from his career point of view, to go back there again.

We were flying home and the take-off was due for 8.00pm. That morning I did some washing and jumped up to put it on the line and came down on my ankle, which collapsed and broke all the tendons in my right leg. In a couple of hours it was huge and unusable! What a thing to do at the eleventh hour. However, we managed, and I was offered a wheelchair to board the aircraft etc which was all rather amusing, for the plane was full of soldiers returning from Korea, and I was the 'wounded' passenger! We went up to the airport at 7.00pm, the children and I full of phenobarb and travel pills and hardly able to keep our eyes open to be told, naturally, that the take-off was delayed. We sat there with our loads (and four baby tortoises that the Squadron boys had given us as a parting present!) until 11.30pm when it was announced that we wouldn't be going until the morning. The result was that we spent the remaining few hours of the night, at RAF expense, in *the* hotel in Nicosia, the Ledra Palace, where we hadn't been able to afford to put our noses into. It was gorgeous too but our stay was far too short, for we were up at 5.00am and eventually took-off at 7.00am.

We had lunch in Malta (wheelchair to boiled liver! I remember) where we met a wing commander we hadn't seen for years. Then on the way home, one of the most gorgeous sights I shall always remember, the Alps, almost pink in the sunset. It was 9.30pm by the time we landed and we had fun with the customs over the tortoises and a large bottle of half drunk Schlivovitz. This was also amusing in itself, for some members of 72 Squadron gave us a bottle, but when we had some visitors from 6 Squadron and showed them our gift without any ulterior motive, they went out and bought us an even bigger and better bottle, for they weren't going to be out done by their rivals.

Eventually we left Stanstead and went by bus to Hendon where we were to spend the rest of the night. One of the new things that hit our eyes were the flashing Belisha beacons at pedestrian crossings, installed while we were overseas. We went to bed about 11.30pm. Why, oh why does air travel have to keep such ghastly hours.

The next day we met Granny for lunch at her club, together with Auntie Dorothy and Uncle Edgar – and me with my limping foot. Then we went on to Eastbourne, where Bess had got us some rooms in the same house as her flat. But oh, I did suffer so from the cold. Ben spent a lot of time going to the Air Ministry to try and sort out our posting and eventually was given command of Acklington, which was to be a fighter station, but not until the end of March. All this was most annoying, for we could have stayed on longer in Cyprus, or wended our way slowly home by boat instead of leaving in a hurry, as we had been given to understand that we were needed urgently!

While we had been in Nicosia, I had written to book some seats for Bertram Mills' Circus and had chosen the coldest day for a century! It was bitter too; even the inside of the railway carriages, which were usually so steamed-up, had ice on them. However, the circus was a tremendous success and we all enjoyed our day immensely.

One day in March we set off for Northumberland, from desert to the frozen north, but I suppose it did us good. The whole of England, from Eastbourne to Newcastle was white – an almost unheard of thing. We drove from Newcastle to Acklington and found a well lit and warmed quarter awaiting for us. A temporary one, for the CO was still installed and we weren't taking over for another two weeks or so.

When Ben finally took over, we moved down on to the camp into one of the most lovely houses we have ever had. We were to spend a very happy two years here in spite of freezing winds, practically no summer, an operation for a gall bladder for me, the loss of Ben's father, and lots of other small off-putting events. It was from here too that Peter left Rossall and started at Cranwell and where we had some amazing animals: a cat which had 'gone' with the house, called Pudding, and one that was soon very dear to us; and a cairn bitch, which was the greatest fun too, called Chicko. She used to play the most amazing games with the cat which caused mats to fly in all directions and eventually had three adorable puppies too. Then Pipyn had endless – yes, endless – guinea pigs! My best cutting scissors were always used when a new run was needed and the wire netting wasn't the right length! Happy days, and I really do think we appreciated our beautiful house. It had eight bedrooms, two bathrooms plus all the other 'offices'. We spent a fortune on central heating but it was worth it.

~ Chapter Six ~

THE FAR EAST

Posted! And great fun too, for we were to be off to Singapore. The station at Acklington gave us a wonderful send-off with parties, presentations and the guard turning out to bid us farewell. These movements very often happen around my birthday and it was in fact on the 18th April 1958, that we left Northumberland. Peter and Penny had left two days before in our Morris Eight, 1937 vintage, that we had bequeathed to Peter. They met us that afternoon at the Regent Palace Hotel for tea and in the evening, as a farewell treat, Ben had got expensive seats for Cinerama and it was with great anticipation that we took our places at 8.00pm. But by 8.30pm Penny and I were back at the hotel feeling very air sick, for the photography was so realistic that we really felt that we were flying! However, we persuaded the others to remain on and enjoy it, and met them afterwards for hot dogs.

The following morning we set off for Waterloo to join the troop train accompanied by Peter with a very stern, set and white face, and me with a very heavy heart at the thought of parting with him. There are times when I have envied my childless friends, when leavings-behind seem almost too much to bear…Yet I wouldn't really have it otherwise. We seated ourselves in a train only to be turned out by a very rude and over efficient sergeant who said we had to wait for the next train. So there was more hanging about and drinking endless cups of tea we didn't need but Ben, in his usual wonderful way, had managed to get us a seat in the restaurant in a quiet corner. Eventually we did leave – a brave Peter waving and me swallowing hard!

At Southampton everything went smoothly and we were soon aboard the Nevassa, a lovely ship. We had lovely cabins and some gorgeous cards from various people. We telephoned Peter at Eastbourne but he had gone to a cinema, and I suppose it was just as well we didn't get hold of him. What would have been the use? When it came time to sail, I duly took my pills and enjoyed the departure. It was when we went down to change for dinner I remarked to Ben that truly they were the best pills ever, for I could hardly feel any movement. This caused a great laugh, for I then discovered that we were anchored because of fog! Anyway, I enjoyed my dinner and just as well, for the next day we three girls were all on starvation diets and remained in bed. I will never forget how those carnations dipped and bobbed with every movement of the ship!

However, misery was not to last too long and two days later we were in Gibraltar. We had a lovely time ashore and it was really warm. The captain told us later that he hated taking his ship into Gib more than anywhere else. However, that didn't worry us. I'm afraid we did all the usual things that tourists do, and bought a lot of trash too. We also had the usual taxi ride up the hill to see the apes. I'm afraid I hate monkeys of any sort; these apes were far too friendly and almost overpowering. Still, there seemed to be plenty of them which was a good thing, for superstition has it that when they leave so do the British... I wonder how long they will survive! The view from the top was magnificent and I would love to go back some day. We sailed at 5.30pm. Ben and I watched a lot of lightening across the sea after dinner, but the next day was beautifully calm and the sea a real Mediterranean blue. That night too, there was a dance on board and Penny was to have her first dance ever – and with the captain! At the time we didn't know it, but Pipyn was to have her first dance too, years later, with another captain in quite a different part of the world.

Each day was very like the other; we were all happy, restful and were wonderfully looked after. I just couldn't believe it was a *troop* ship after my previous experience. On 27th April we called at Limassol to drop some troops and dashed on to the Suez Canal as the captain was in a hurry to get well forward in the queue and we got there at 6.45pm. We anchored, but I was weary and went to bed early and missed the gully-gully men etc. We started through the canal at 11.20pm, which was a shame as we then travelled through most of it by night. When we awoke at 6.00am, it was still there and we travelled through it all day until 5.15pm. The sight of the desert does something to all the Boults, we love it so, and of course Ben was able to tell me so much about the canal as he had spent almost five years near it and on it, at the beginning of his service career.

The next day it was really warm and it got hotter and hotter until we reached Aden on the 1st May. There was a nice breeze blowing there and we enjoyed the place very much. The girls went ashore with some other people and went swimming, while we went to drinks at an RAF quarter with an air commodore and were back for dinner. We sailed again at 10.15pm.

Next stop: Colombo – on Penny's birthday! Poor Pip had a high temperature and tonsillitis so I stayed on board with her while the others went sightseeing. Pipyn was really bad and was moved to the ship's hospital where she was most unhappy, poor poppet! Ben's back was also bad, so the voyage was ending on a little unhappy note.

Singapore on the 11th May, and the Tippers were there to meet us armed with masses of orchids! Somehow the end of a voyage is always an anti-climax – who said, "How much nicer it was to travel, than to arrive"? Eventually we got ashore and went to the Grand Hotel which was really a sort of transit hotel for people waiting for quarters. Sometimes the waiting seemed to us endless, though we were comparatively lucky and were only there for seven weeks. The hotel was only 'Grand' by name and at first we were so miserable, and longed to go home! As time wore on we began to become more acclimatised, make new friends, joined the Singapore Club, and bought a car etc.

Singapore at first reminded us in many ways of Baghdad, not the modern parts, but perhaps the smells more than anything! It was a fascinating place: the washing hanging from windows on bamboo poles; the tri-shaws; the colourful fruit stalls; along the roadside palm trees; tropical flowers in every colour; and best of all, Chinese food! We got to love it, and whenever we had an excuse we would go to Bedok Corner for a meal. Here one sat outside, weather permitting (and it nearly always did), and ate endless dishes of varying foods, each course washed down by delicious tea. The table was laid with a beautiful white cloth but by the time we had tried, successfully or otherwise, to pick up such things as crabs' thumbs from a centre bowl with chopsticks, the cloth was well and truly mottled. As the Chinese regard the dirty state of a cloth as a compliment, one never had to worry about dropping anything. The meal ended by one being supplied with gorgeous hot towels, dipped in eau de cologne as often as not. One only left when one just couldn't manage another grain of fried rice or another drop of tea.

Ben was at Head Quarters Far East Air Force, at Changi, and was Chairman of the Overseas Establishment Committee, a job which entailed a lot of travelling. The girls went to school at Changi too (fourteen miles from Singapore and notorious for its prison where so many of our soldiers, sailors and airmen suffered such terrible things during the War at the hands of the Japanese. The prison was built to hold six hundred, but during the War there were fourteen thousand British there at one time).

We eventually moved into a very nice house at Lloyd Leas, a bungalow which was only to be temporary until we moved again into Changi itself. It was here in this house that I wanted to celebrate our unpacking by buying some gorgeous flowers and I asked the greengrocer, Mr G. Oh, to bring me something special, and he did. At least he thought he did, for he produced some very mouldy looking golden rod! These were never my favourite flower, but he thought the 'English mem would be welly pleased' – and I had visualised lovely orchids! However, I managed to muster a smile and take them with a good grace, I hope. Penny and I also cooked our first Chinese chicken here for a dinner party and were horrified to discover that what we thought was stuffing was merely an uncleaned crop – no wonder it tasted gritty!

Later we moved to 68 East Church Road. I had thought the quarter at Acklington lovely, but this was heaven. Heaven complete with a guardian angel, for we took on a magnificent Chinese servant and amah; Loh Kai Tong and Boh Tai. He was silent as a mouse; always there, yet never in the way; and able to produce a meal for ten or two, early or late. Whilst she coped with the most enormous wash each day and was only about five foot tall. Such happy, happy days – nothing to do but the flowers and the tapestry! We had a gay social life too and Ben managed to get a lot of sailing and bought a half share of a Snipe called naturally, Blue Peter. Penny had left school by now and was going into Singapore every day doing shorthand and typing, and also had a bash at modelling. Her experiences on the way to work were often amusing. She had to go by bus and, as the drivers were paid by the number of journeys they could make in a day, speed was the operative word. She would often have her heels pecked by some hungry fowl or duck belonging to some Chinese woman going to market. Once she said she couldn't think for the noise that a large croaking frog made on the lap of a fellow traveller beside her.

We did a lot of sightseeing too and got to know Singapore well I think – such different things to see. One of them was Tiger Balm Gardens, a garden really filled with extraordinary statues, models etc, in the most vivid colours depicting all sorts of things. It was a place where something is forever being built on the instructions of the departed owner, who said that work must always go on to ensure him a comfy resting place in the hereafter. Then there was the Street of Birds with its endless, endless cages of birds of every colour size and description. My dear old mother was appalled when I told her about them and she asked if I couldn't let them all go! There were lots of wonderful shops with so many glorious pieces of jade etc.

Oh yes, and the House of Jade with its fabulous collection. This escaped being deported to Japan during the war because it was one of the first things that the Japanese confiscated. The collection was placed on the docks at the bottom of the pile of a tremendous amount of loot, but was never removed. The jade is quite wonderful, all colours, and the owner has refused fantastic offers from other would-be collectors. We also went out to the Kranji War Memorial which was a wonderful place, beautifully cared for and the sort of place, as Pipyn so rightly said, that makes one want to whisper. On from there to Johor Bahru, across the causeway into Malaya. Here we saw the most beautiful mosque which towered over the most awful little zoo, a place of minute cages and miserable animals – it depressed me beyond words.

On one occasion, after Pipyn had had her tonsils out, we went on local leave up to a hill station called Fraser's Hill. Loh Tong got us up very early at 4.30am. We left the house before sunrise and had a most lovely drive up to Kuala Lumpar through endless rubber trees and oil palm plantations. At Kuala Lumpar we stayed the night at the Railway Hotel, a railway hotel to beat all others, for it looks more like a mosque or sultan's palace than anything else. The next morning, we went up the hill. One has to time one's arrival, for the road is closed at different times of the day to allow down-coming traffic, there being single file traffic only. It is a wonderful climb up the hillside and as one gets higher and higher the foliage changes and there are lovely tree ferns. The mountains in the distance are quite blue and seem to roll on forever. One wonders how on earth the Communist terrorists were ever defeated.

At the top is a village which could have been transplanted from many places in England, together with a pub and a nine hole golf course. We had a bungalow that we shared with another couple, and a personal servant who did all the cooking and ordering so that it was a complete rest. There were lovely wood fires at night and every conceivable kind of flower. Here, where there are no newspapers and where one could live quite apart from the rest of the world, it was easy to see why people awoke one morning to find that the Japanese had arrived and that the War was upon them. We lazed our days away, Ben playing golf most days and us walking with him. One afternoon he said he would take us for a short jungle walk. Walk we did, and about two hours later emerged in the sunlight! I must admit I was a nuisance, chiefly because I didn't like being shut-in by such high trees, and because my wild imagination prompted me to think every creaking leaf was caused by the movement of some wild animal. I was convinced we were lost and would just be posted as 'missing'.

In February 1958, we had a trip to Hong Kong. The return journey cost Ben one pound each for Pip and myself – quite unbelievable! Penny went up by sea with some friends and had a rotten voyage, for they had a force nine gale the entire time. She was violently ill and when we met her in Kowloon, she still looked pale! We had an uneventful flight calling in at Saigon and taking about seven hours from A to B. When we left Saigon it was hot, but at the other end we were glad of our coats – it was most refreshing. We were going to stay with a cousin of Ben's, Hardress Waller, a Colonel in the RA and who was stationed at Fanling, about five miles from the Bamboo Curtain. He had sent a car to meet us and we had a delightful drive arriving at their sweet, pink house in time for tea. The next morning it was like an English spring day and we went to Kowloon by train and did such a lot of shopping.

Kowloon is quite fascinating, so colourful, so crowded and everything so amazingly cheap! Gorgeous flowers were everywhere and everybody trying to sell something. The refugee problem was immense and, although slum clearance had begun and had progressed rapidly, there was still nothing like enough accommodation. Each room was shared by a family of about fourteen and they had to sleep in shifts. It was home again by train, and we fell into bed by 10.00pm. The next morning Ben went to Kowloon, and Pipyn and I had a lazy day together – she catching endless butterflies.

The following day we were up at the crack of dawn as we were off to see the Duke of Edinburgh inspect a parade in Kowloon – 3,179 men on parade and a very impressive sight. Unfortunately the clouds were down, so there could not be a fly past. On Sunday we went with our host and hostess over to Victoria on Hong Kong Island. There are continuous ferries between the island and the mainland and it was a beautiful sight to see HMS Britannia at anchor and junks of all sizes ploughing to and fro with sails patched in so many places. All the ships were dressed overall, and it was something we will always remember.

On the Sunday our hosts took us for a sightseeing tour. It really was a lovely day and we saw some beautiful views and sights that we shall treasure always. We had lunch aboard a houseboat in Aberdeen Bay. Sea Food House it was called, and one had to get to it by sampan which was great fun as the movement of the little boat was something quite unto itself. When aboard, one looked over the side of the boat and chose a particular fish. There were many fish of various sizes and beautiful colours which were swimming around in baskets suspended just below the water. The chosen one was then killed and cooked while you waited and drank endless cups of delicious Chinese tea.

Aberdeen Bay is just crammed to full capacity with junks, mile upon mile of them, and one can step from junk to junk and never touch the water at all. They are the homes for thousands of people and I am told that some of the fishermen never do set foot on land. As you can imagine, everything takes place aboard these little ships: babies are born, people die; the washing of persons and linen is done by hanging over the side; and all refuse is just dumped, not a very savoury thought when feeding on the fish that had been caught there. I found it rather amusing(?) too when we girls retired to the comfort station at the stern of the restaurant, to find that the seat in question was just a round hole with a sheer drop into the water! When in Hong Kong…

Soon we had to return to the heat of Singapore. We were sad to leave but felt much refreshed after our two weeks in the cool. Inevitably we piled into the waiting Hastings – and piled out again, for there was an electrical fault. After about two hours all was well and we duly took-off, arriving at Changi at about 7.00pm.

The next eight months at Changi simply fled. Many of our friends had left. It always seems to be that when one first arrives at a station one knows no one, then towards the end of a tour it is the same, for all the friends one has made, leave before one. We had a lot of farewell parties and soon our turn came to give one. At the end of November 1959 we sailed in the Oxfordshire for home. There were lots of people to see us off and so many beautiful baskets of orchids. We really felt so sad, but we had the reunions with Peter and Penny to look forward to (Penny had flown home earlier) and, we thought, the joy of settling down in England – plus the excitement of a beautiful new Wolsey 15/60 we had ordered to meet the ship at Southampton, Ben having 'burst' some of his gratuity on it. When we sailed it simply pelted and one very sweet remark made by some great friends of ours will always remain in my mind, "When angels depart, the heavens weep" – one more thing to be treasured in our hearts.

This time I went ashore in Colombo and of course Pipyn came too. We hired a car for the day, having gone from the ship to shore in the RAF launch. First we visited a jeweller and saw endless uncut stones which seemed very disappointing in their nakedness. We bought some opals, two zircons and a lovely rose coloured stone of no value but of great beauty. Then the jeweller gave Pipyn a small star sapphire which proved to be the most valuable stone of the lot when we took them to be mounted in England. We then drove around Colombo, visiting shrines and seeing a huge and very impressive golden Buddha, the monks in their yellow robes seeming to tone in so well with the whole setting.

On to Mount Lavinia for lunch, where the crows are so tame they come on to the veranda and can be fed by hand. There was a lovely view from the veranda of stretches of sand and palm trees, and it was here that a lot of the scenes for the film *The Bridge over the River Kwai* were shot, I believe. There was a snake charmer on the lawn, but as usual, his snakes seemed to be very weary and had to be poked into life. On the way back to the ship we bought some gorgeous flowers and I had noticed how the weather had changed. To my horror when we reached the docks, there was a strong wind blowing and the launch which was to take us back to the ship was bobbing alarmingly. One moment it was above the sides of the jetty, and the next it was feet below. I am an awful coward and was quite prepared to decide to spend the rest of my days in Colombo rather than make a jump for it. A decision which was strengthened when an airman missed the leaping vessel, landed in the drink and had to be fished out – luckily unharmed. Anyway, I made it in the end by the guidance of others, for I was much too frightened to look and had my eyes tightly shut!

We had lovely days at sea until we once more reached Aden. The only excitement being an emergency call from a Norwegian tramper in mid-Indian Ocean for medical help. The Oxfordshire went alongside and the sick seaman was taken on board and was found to be suffering from severe food poisoning. We arrived at Aden on St Andrew's day, so we all decided to see if we could buy any tartan for the festivities that night. Of course there was none to be had, but we had great fun trying to describe to the Arabs what we wanted; the nearest we got was gingham. We took a taxi and went to Crater to buy a small pair of pliers that Ben needed. They were the most expensive pliers possible, I should think, by the time one had paid an exorbitant fee for the taxi. That night we had a real Scottish 'do' and it was great fun. Everyone of all nationalities entered into the spirit and Ben, who hasn't a drop of Scottish blood in his veins and is only scotch by absorption, borrowed a kilt and was christened McBen from the Glen.

On to the canal once more, and a delay of thirty-six hours because of a sandstorm. This was sad, for once more we eventually passed through most of it during the night. Pipyn and I did have a little weep when we saw the last of the desert though – for all of us, there is nowhere that we love better. Then it was on to Gibraltar at night, where we were not allowed ashore this time. But when we rounded Finistaire... to bed, to bed as there was a severe gale blowing and a lot of people succumbed. The first I knew about it was to find two men in our cabin at midnight shutting the portholes. However, it only(!) lasted two days, but it did mean that we were twenty-four hours late arriving at Southampton. The captain said it was one of the worst storms he remembered, so I didn't feel too bad by my non-appearance at meals.

~ Chapter Seven ~

WEST AFRICA

Southampton: dull, wet and cold. It was such a contrast somehow, but we were full of excitement and the first thing we did was to ring Penny, who was almost in tears at the end of the phone. We drove straight up to Camberley where she was working and collected her for lunch. It was soon that we discovered that part of her tearfulness over the telephone was due to the fact that she was unhappy over her engagement and wanted to break it off. She had become engaged while we were still in Singapore to an army officer. We had given them our blessing although we were not really happy about things, for we felt they had met in Hong Kong under very romantic circumstances and didn't really know each other.

We had been offered a quarter for our last three months in the service at Hawarden, near Chester and although at first it seemed cold, lonely and surrounded by empty houses, we soon got to love it and felt so at home. Penny and Peter came to join us, but Peter went off to Switzerland with some others from Cranwell. The rest of us had a very happy Christmas, being joined by Granny. Soon after the New Year began, we went down to London and then on to Southampton to meet my mother whom I had not seen for seventeen years and who was going to live in England to be near us. All the time though, Ben was answering endless advertisements, two hundred in all, for jobs. The only ones he could possibly have had were in London, St Helen's or Manchester and we just decided that we couldn't bear to live in such civilisation. At the same time he was attending a rehabilitation course at the Commercial College in Liverpool, and was deciding daily that trade and commerce just wasn't for him. He could not bear to join the rat race – but what to do? Then an offer arrived from the Crown Agents of a job as Administration Officer with the Sierra Leone government. We looked it up on the map and found that it really was rather far away, but it would be good fun to go. But what about my mother? What about Pipyn's schooling? We had tried to get her into a boarding school but to no avail, no places. Then Peter dropped another bombshell – he wanted to leave Cranwell!

Ben was summoned to the COs presence at Cranwell to try to persuade Peter to remain on. However, Ben thought that Peter was right in his decision as, to put it in a nutshell, Peter felt he was doing something negative, for if there was a war we would all be in it anyway. Peter said that he would rather be doing something that would be useful to society, such as being a planter. Ben then went on to London to see the Crown Agents as a decision had to be made soon. That night he rang me to have one more chat about things. In the meantime my mother had decided she couldn't stand the cold and would have to return to South Africa – one obstacle off the list. Then Ben thought he would ring the school to use his powers of persuasion and the headmistress said, "What an extraordinary thing you should ring at this moment, for I have just had a cancellation and we can take Pipyn." More and more things fell into line and before we knew what had happened, we boarded the Apapa in Liverpool and set sail for Freetown, on 14th April 1960. We three that is, Penny coming with us while Pipyn was at school in Eastbourne where Peter got himself a temporary job doing the accounts at a garage while in turn, answering endless advertisements for jobs as his father had done months before.

Once more my birthday was on board! As we got nearer the African coast the weather got hotter and stickier and at that time, the ship was not air conditioned. We called in at Bathurst in the Gambia, where we went ashore. It was simply lovely to have the smell of Africa in one's nostrils once more. We loved Bathurst: a fascinating market; some gorgeous bougainvillaea; and above all the women, who were dressed magnificently with head-dresses which had to be seen to be believed, gossamer and silver thread, bright colours, brocades and flowing robes – really gorgeous.

Two days later we arrived at Freetown which was very, very, hot and damp, but from the sea the coastline is quite beautiful and very reminiscent of Hong Kong, but there the similarity ends. No docks are ever beautiful, and it was not until we reached the top of Hill Station above the town that we could really take in the beauty of the seascape. We were met by a government official, who saw us through customs and took us to the government rest house where we had to stay until a house could be found for us. April is about the worst time to arrive in West Africa and I can remember lying on my bed at the transit camp dripping, with no fans and no water in the shower, and thinking, "I just can't stay here." However, we soon became acclimatised and once the rains came, the water shortage ceased. Before the rains however, there are the most alarming, noisy and brilliant storms where the lightning was continuous at times and the thunder really deafening. Ben found that the pace was very slow and life was frustrating at times, but he soon slowed down to keep in time and we got to love the life, especially the beaches. The beaches are, or must be, some of the most beautiful in the world, and every afternoon after work we used to go swimming, and most weekends we picnicked after church.

Church, the cathedral, was an eye opener and put many congregations to shame. We had been attending services in Chester Cathedral before we left where there was only a mere handful of people each Sunday, but in Freetown the cathedral was packed each Sunday at 9.30am and on special occasions there was standing room only. The normal congregation is about five hundred and the service is sung with great gusto and the people really enjoy the singing. The Te Deum etc was sung much faster that we were accustomed to, but in some ways it was much nicer like that. On the first Sunday of the month the sidesmen all wear morning coats and everyone is always in their best clothes. Entire families worship together and we have witnessed several amusing situations. One was when the pew in front of us was occupied by a family of about eight, ranging from a newly born babe to a grandmother. During the Venite the babe was passed along the line to granny who changed its nappy and then passed it back to its mother before the end of the singing, and we all sat down as if nothing had happened. Another time when we sat down for the sermon, which sometimes were long, a small boy tore out the front page of his hymn book and stuffed it in one ear; tore out the back page and stuffed it in the other; folded his arms; and sat back and dreamed the minutes away gazing as if in full attention.

After about ten days we moved into a house which we were to caretake for three months, a lovely double storied building in Brookfields. However, we had only been in about six weeks when we were very badly burgled, or 'tiefed' as it was known here. We three went to bed early and at about 5.30am I awoke and said to Ben, "I'm going to put the light on and 'flit' as I am being bitten," whereupon the front door slammed! Ben leapt out of bed, and found the stairs littered with things from his wallet. We then discovered that the dressing table drawers had been removed from our bedroom and Penny's, and had been taken into the drawing room and sorted for valuables. The thieves had been under her mosquito net and taken her watch from beside her bed, which she had a habit of taking off at night. They had also been under our mosquito net and taken my handbag, which I had beside my bed, and contained my only valuable piece of jewellery – a five diamond ring worth three hundred pounds and an heirloom! The thieves had drunk all the beer in the fridge, taken the food and, just for the fun of it, had left the empties on the veranda. We rang the police who came very quickly, but said no fingerprints were clear enough to be of any use. This seemed odd to us when one would have thought the beer cans would have had plenty on them. Endless other things of course were missing: material I had bought for curtains; small jewellery; and above all, a lovely photograph of Penny which we had taken in Singapore. We discovered that the thieves had got in by putting a small piccaninny in through the tiny lavatory window in the downstairs cloakroom and he had unbolted the front door.

The amazing thing is that we are all very light sleepers and are all equally convinced that some form of hypnotism or ju-ju must have been used. Ben says he sensed all the time that something odd was going on, but he just couldn't pull himself out of a dead sleep. The creepy thing to me was that someone had been in and out of our room! Incidentally we are all firm believers in ju-ju, it's quite an indescribable thing, but there *is* something and of course, most Africans are convinced of its power. It is well known that if someone is told by a witch doctor that he is going to die as a result of a ju-ju, he will just sit down and slowly die, although doctors may have examined him and found him to be in perfect health. The Creoles, or aristocracy, do not believe in such things and are therefore immune to threats. When I asked our steward how they made ju-ju, he went into a long story about taking some innards from a newly dead person (whether the death was by natural causes or 'helped', he didn't state). These ingredients are then put into a pot, cooked and chanted over, and then a small child is taken towards them. If the child makes no noise when burnt by the fire, then it is good ju-ju. If it 'hollers', then it's no good, and they start all over again! A good story anyway.

While we were in this house Penny fell in love! I mean really in love, with an awfully nice man and we were very happy about it. It all came to a climax one afternoon when they came home together, Nigel having collected her from the office, and we felt something was in the wind.

Penny said, "Come and have a shower with me Mummy," which I thought was a little odd at 4.30pm! but I duly left the two men talking together on the veranda. Poor Nigel, he was dying to ask Ben if he might marry Penny, and had just blurted out the question when a car rolled up and someone shouted, "I'm going to Murraytown, are you interested?" Ben dropped Nigel, came to the bathroom and said to me, "First things first, do you want any fish? And, oh yes, Nigel wants to marry Penny!" All this time Nigel was in a tizzy wondering if the answer was going to be 'no'. However, we were all delighted and decided we must celebrate somehow. All we could suggest was 'dinner' at the rest house, at the time there being no hotel in Freetown. I remember the warm wine and somehow, above all, how all the mustard pots had tired, dry mustard on the spoons and on their sides. Nevertheless, it was a lovely evening and we were all so very happy and thrilled.

From then on the wedding was the main topic of discussion as you can imagine. They decided on 18th October as the date, and were to be married in the cathedral. Nigel was due for leave then and that would be their honeymoon. He had been in Freetown for some time and had endless friends and the invitation list grew longer and longer. There was nowhere to buy lovely undies or clothes, so everything had to come from England, including the head-dress which arrived two days before the wedding, after cables had been sent backwards and forwards. We did find a Paris trained Iraqi dressmaker to make Penny's dress. It really was beautiful, white brocade with a silver thread and she was the calmest bride I have known – and looked so lovely. Pipyn was the only bridesmaid and Peter came out for the wedding. Poor Penny! All her plans for a bouquet fell down as, during the evening, there was a storm and not one flower survived, so she carried a white prayer book. Pipyn, in white broderie anglaise over blue, carried blue hydrangeas.

It was an unfortunate pre-wedding night as Penny's friend, who had been doing her hair and had promised to set it in a special way on *the* day, was admitted to hospital with suspected appendicitis! We did manage to get an appointment at Henry Ducks and what ever happened, it wouldn't have mattered as Penny was glowing with such happiness and looked beautiful in her radiance. Her calmness and deep feeling of great joy simply shone from her lovely blue eyes.

The reception was held at Hill Station Club which had been transformed by a willing band of friends: carpets lent by Dottie Wise; arrangements of bougainvillaea and other gorgeous tropical flowers, done beautifully by Audrey Mackenzie and Cherry Preston amongst others; a lovely cake made by an army wife; and bottles of champagne completed the arrangement.

The wedding ceremony was in the cathedral and I had done the flowers in the morning. They were married by the canon, Canon King, who did everything so charmingly and the whole service was most moving. One slight cause of amusement was the pronunciation of their names, Pener-lope and Niggell, but somehow it all added to it and perhaps allowed us not to be just that much too serious, and so let the tears begin to well-up. It was all very moving and the cathedral was packed. As you can imagine, lots of photographs were taken at the door and later, and they still give us the greatest joy whenever we look at them. After the reception, Penny changed into a liberty silk dress and she and Nigel flew from Hastings to Lungi where they spent the night, before going on to London via Paris. Frantic messages from the pilot managed to get them to Hastings just in time to take-off and land at the other end before dark, for of course, there were no night landing aids.

A wonderful day was over and we were all tired but so happy. On Sunday we went to church to give heartfelt thanks for so many blessings, and then picnicked all day at Kent, about forty miles along the coast, relaxing before clearing up the vases and tubs of flowers the following morning. When we got home we had a frantic message from Penny saying she had left her inoculation papers behind and would we please get them over to Lungi. This we did by Ben putting them in the hands of an airport official going over on the early morning ferry to meet an aircraft.

Peter left on the Wednesday and it was a sad farewell as he was off to Malaya for three and a half years. It was what he wanted, so that eased the parting. Soon we were busy preparing for Christmas and then had the joy of meeting Granny, who came out for two months. In the meantime we had moved house for the third time, up to Hill Station to Number 14 which was a lovely old rambling wooden house. It had no view, which was a great shame, but after being painted was very nice and much cooler than the little house in Brookfields.

Penny and Nigel spent a day with us on their return to Accra, sailing out in the ship of that name – what fun it was! There was so much to talk about and for Poo to show us, such as her lovely clothes and jewellery. We went back to the ship early so that she could let us see all her things. It was lucky we did, for when we arrived at the docks the customs said that they had been informed that Nigel was smuggling diamonds! So all their crates were searched; everything thrown on the dockside, pictures ripped open, ginger jars emptied etc; and then things were thrown back into the crates in any sort of way, with a pile of packing left on the quayside. The captain kept the ship waiting an hour and a half and tempers were frayed. Of course he wasn't smuggling and after BAT had lodged a strong complaint at the treatment they had suffered, the customs apologised and said it was the wrong Brown! Meanwhile the other Brown, no doubt, had left by air quite unmolested with his loot.

From then on Ben was frantically busy as independence was to be declared on 27th April 1961 and he was involved in a lot of the preparation for it. We had planned to go on leave just afterwards and had been assured we would not be wanted in connection with the Queen's visit in November 1961. When all our plans were made, he was asked to lunch by his minister and, after much wine and liqueurs, was asked if he would after all agree to extend his tour! The wine however had had the opposite effect to that anticipated – and he spoke his mind! However, when he got back to the office he thought that perhaps he had been a little unwise. So he rang up, apologised, and agreed to stay on condition we had some mid-tour leave. In the meantime he had made two hundred pounds on the Stock Exchange (the one and only time) and we decided to blow it on a sea trip to Ghana to see Penny and Nigel, who had given us the wonderful news that we were to be grandparents the following March.

We went down on the Apapa, but when we arrived at Takoradi there was a dockers' strike so we had to go ashore on lighters; climbing down a ship's side on swinging ladders is not my favourite pastime! Pipyn had flown on ahead of us, and had already been with Penny for three weeks. When she landed at Accra it was found that no one had thought of getting her a visa, although we had asked about it and had been told that it wasn't necessary. However a small tip from Nigel, and the visa was forgotten! We spent the day with the Teales', Nigel's friends, and that night flew to Accra arriving after dark on a flight which I enjoyed but Ben didn't, as he knew peculiar things were happening – we did have about three shots at getting down!

It was wonderful to see 'Les Browns' again. They had such a lovely house and a happy home, and Penny ran it so efficiently without any fuss. Poor child, she was being and feeling horribly sick! They spoilt us of course. We had a lovely ten days of late mornings in air conditioning,

Rhodesia, 1936

Ben after the accident at Mersa Matruh, 1936
Side view of the beard

Marshall Symons OBE, London, 1937
Peggy's father, born 1886

Dorothy Michell (née Williams), 1910
Peggy's mother born 13 Feb 1884

Rhodesia, 1915

Rhodesia, 1935

Umtali, Rhodesia, 1937

Shawanae, Rhodesia, 1937

Umkomaas, South Africa, 1933

Mermaid's Pool, Rhodesia, 1935

Rhodesia, 1937

Ben with stepbrother/sister Richard and Val. Margate, 1938

London, 2nd April 1938
At the wedding reception

Wellesbourne, late 1940s
Group Captain Ben Boult

Hanover Square, London 1938
High Commissioner Llandigan O'Keefe,

St George's Chapel, London, 1938
The Guard of Honour bar one were killed in the War

Peter and Penny. Bourton-on-the-Water, 1947

Scotland, 1950s

Penny and Peter. Rhodesia, 1943

Dunsfold, 1944
180 Squadron B-25 Mitchell Bombers

England, 1940s
Ben receiving DFC from George VI

Habbaniya, Iraq, 1953-1955
Chief Announcer and Agony Aunt

Iraq/Iran Border, 1955
Charlie in the background

Rowanduz, Iraq, 1955

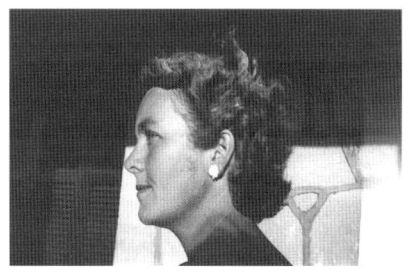

Habbaniya, Iraq 1954

Habbaniya, Iraq, 1955

Iraq/Iran Border, 1955
Persian WO at fort

RAF Habbaniya, Iraq, 1955

Kyrenia, Cyprus, 1956

Acklington, Northumberland, 1958

68 East Church Road, Changi, Singapore, 1958

Cyprus, 1957

Howarden, 1960
Pipyn, Peter and Penny

South Caicos, 1967
Liam McGuire presenting the regatta trophy

Aunt Flo 1887-1978. England, 1977

Tuirnaig, Loch Ewe, 1970s

Uncle John 1890-1977. Devon, 1976

St Helier, Jersey, 1979
Pipyn and grandson J-P

The Croft, Devon, 1970s
Uncle John and Marshall who died in 1982

Grandson Adrian. Conifers, Devon, 1975

Robin Hood's Bay, 1994

Lewdown, Devon, 1964

Lewdown, Devon, 1964

Robin Hood's Bay, 1994

Pipyn. Halfpenny House, 1990s

picnics, drives; and during one evening at a most amusing night club, I saw my first and largest ever 'diamond' tummy button on a belly dancer.

We enjoyed Accra very much and admired the well laid out streets and the cheerful, helpfulness of the people. The financial 'squeeze' had not started properly and the shops appeared to be full of things, but all that was to change dramatically within a few months. Red China was much in evidence and we went to an exhibition that was being held by them – very good too, it was. By road at dawn to Takoradi this time, and all three of us went back to Freetown on the Apapa.

We felt so much better for our leave and Ben was to need his extra energy, as he was given some almost impossible tasks over Her Majesty's visit. He had to open, run and close down a hotel for one hundred press and radio representatives. This was an awful job when starting from scratch with no time in hand and so little available in Freetown. Even the fish knives and forks arrived on the same plane as the first guests!

Her Majesty was superb, and we had some wonderful invitations to functions. Seeing HMS Britannia slide into place, gleaming from stem to stern was most thrilling; and then the Queen coming ashore in the palest blue, was something I shall never forget. We the spectators, were hot and dripping and mopping endlessly and she, who was doing all the work, looked cool and never once gave anyone the impression that she was feeling the heat, which she must have done tremendously. We went to garden parties and to the Ball where Ben was an extra aide-de-camp which was an honour. At the Ball the Queen wore a fairy-tale dress of red lace and a gorgeous tiara and we danced next to her and the Duke on several occasions. She was obviously enjoying herself as she stayed much later than expected. The people of Sierra Leone were much to be congratulated on their behaviour, it was beyond criticism. We have heard that their good manners were much appreciated by royalty and there was no crushing or crowding around the royal couple, such as marred occasions in other African countries.

An amusing story is told of the Duke when one morning his African aide-de-camp was standing at the State House drawing room when His Royal Highness came in, "Jenks," he called. "Sir?" answered the a-de-c, "How de body," asked Prince Philip. A question he had been longing to ask in the local Creole dialect for sometime. During their stay the Queen and Duke travelled up-country and at one durbah met all the chiefs who came up the dais steps to greet Her Majesty. One Paramount Chief named Torbor was seen by the Queen to be much older than all the others, in fact he was the oldest of all the chiefs by many years, and when he approached she went *down* to meet him. The crowd roared their appreciation at such a gesture and we have since heard that that move did more to enhance her popularity than anything else.

We were sad when the visit came to an end, with HMS Britannia gliding by King Tom landing stage ablaze with lights, and the band on board playing the Sierra Leone national anthem. It was most moving and hardly anyone had a dry eye.

Some months later, in fact after we had returned from leave, Ben was leaving the office at lunch time when someone across the road whistled after him with the peculiar hissing sound that they make to attract attention instead of saying, "Oi," and when he stopped, a rather ragged messenger handed him an envelope and said, "Sign here." Ben then threw the parcel into the back of the car and when he got home we opened it – an Independence Medal! Having once been presented in the field with a Royal Air Force Cross award by King George VI, it seemed a somewhat odd way of being presented with a medal, but all the same we are very proud of it.

A week after the Queen had departed we left on leave, arriving home three days before Christmas. Ben had caught a chill and was most unwell. We went to Holbrook House Hotel near Wincanton, spending one night at another hotel en route, at Kidderminster. At the hotel Granny, and George and Helen Church were waiting for us, and gave us a great welcome. We had been given a room at the top of the house which was bitterly cold. We were rather miserable and Ben was in bed for several days.

We did manage to enjoy Christmas though, and after it we left for Polruan-by-Fowey where we had rented a cottage which was very sweet and we were very happy. We spent our days driving around the west of England searching for a house to buy and we looked at endless 'desirable residences', most of which bore no resemblance to their descriptions. We did find one however, near Torrington, which we liked very much. It was one of twelve semi-detached houses (which sounds awful!) made from an old stable block on an estate at St Giles-in-the-Wood. But nothing would go right for us as we couldn't raise the money etc and in the end, we had to give up the idea of living there. That left us with about seven weeks leave, so we decide to have *one* more look and then we would give up until the following leave. It was on our way up to London that we saw a lovely little thatched cottage for sale and wrote to the agents asking if they had any others on their books. They sent us particulars for seven cottages, and one morning we got up early to view the lot. It was the first cottage that we came to that we fell in love with, it felt right somehow. Although we did go to see most of the others, our heart had been lost to Hayne Barton, and everything simply fell into line in the most incredible way. Within three weeks we had moved in – quite fantastic!

We had three weeks in the cottage before leaving for Sierra Leone and it was the greatest fun unpacking things that had been in store for years and years. The first day we really viewed the cottage it was sleeting hard and conditions couldn't have been much worse, but somehow we felt as if we belonged. There was much more in that feeling than we knew, for three years later we found out through some cousins of mine in America that my Great Aunt Anne and Great Uncle Henry had been born in that same hamlet of Stowford in 1879! We looked up their names in the church register. Another coincidence was that the same Sunday that we did so, we were asked to lunch time drinks and met the grandson of the rector that christened them.

It was quite extraordinary the effect some houses had on us when we were looking through them. Pipyn and I were particularly sensitive I think, Ben being a much braver soul! Some of the old vicarages gave us the creeps and in one or two we had to remain outside. There was one vicarage however, that we all three loved near Land's End, but we couldn't go ahead with trying to buy it, as it was to be such a long procedure. Funnily enough we were to meet someone almost four years later who had been staying in that same house, and who we discovered quite by chance when having an after dinner drink in the middle of Africa.

Our cottage was quite heavenly: three hundred and fifty years old; thatched; beamed, but not too heavily; with a big enough garden to enable us to have a small orchard; quiet; in the country yet accessible from the A30 and within easy reach of the shops. Anyone would think I was trying to sell it! We have had such happy times under its warm thatch. I love to let my imagination run riot by picturing coaches and horses etc in the olden days, and wondering so much what exciting events took place within those very walls – what stories it would tell!

This was a really wonderful leave that we had, for in March our first grandson was born. We went up to Yorkshire to meet Nigel's parents and I must say, it was with some trepidation that we did so, for none of us knew what to expect. I am sure that they were dreading our visit too! Anyway, we all took to each other immediately, had the nicest weekend one could imagine and were sorry to leave. We couldn't change our plans to remain longer for several reasons: one being a heavy snow warning; and the other was that we felt that we might be delayed for weeks if we didn't get away as planned. Dominic Roy de Warrenne was born in Accra, Ghana and the cable announcing his arrival on 9th March 1962, arrived as we were due at Whitby – so what could have been a more promising beginning to our visit?

After Easter we sailed once more on the Apapa but this time, for the very fist time in our lives, we had a *home* of our own to return to, and that made all the difference to our tour. Our tour flew by rapidly and we returned in May of the following year, 1963, being met at the ship (Accra, this time) by a lovely little Mini Traveller, an Austin Countryman in fact. To the cottage we sped, calling in for tea at the Spuds en route, and what heaven it was to be in our lovely home again!

After a week of sorting out and unpacking, Ben went up to London to collect his mother to bring her down for a short holiday. They were driving to the RAF Club for supper just after a terrific cloudburst when, in the maze of the Hyde Park new road system which was under construction, Ben took a wrong turning. He applied the brakes too soon as he realised that he was entering a one way street – but nothing happened! Unfortunately, the brakes were wet and simply wouldn't grip, so they slid into an oncoming car at about ten miles an hour. His mother, who weighed about five stone, was thrown against the dashboard and sustained concussion and had both legs broken below the knees. Poor Ben! How terrible he felt and how afraid he was that he had killed his mother. An ambulance was soon on the scene and she was rushed into St George's Hospital where she spent several weeks in much pain and her mind slightly affected. Eventually we managed to get her taken down to Tavistock Hospital where we could visit her every day. Her face was so black, blue and green that her niece, Margaret Earee, fainted when she saw her on a visit to the hospital.

Eventually the wonderful day came when we were able to collect her from the hospital and have her at the cottage where we could spoil her and try to make up a little for all she had suffered. She truly was wonderful, for she made an extraordinary recovery, walking without a stick and was as bright as a bee. The weeks for me were very trying at times, for my head was playing up and I wasn't feeling well in the whole, but it was the least I could do.

Poor Ben had been searching for a job, but it seemed that nothing would turn up. He made up his mind that we would return to Sierra Leone and somehow break the news to his mother, who was at that time still in hospital. He left us in the car while he went into the house agent to arrange the letting of the cottage and came out with a job! Our joy was tremendous. He was to organise and run an abattoir at Hatherleigh. The pay wasn't very good but we thought we could manage, and anyway it was something. He began on 18th August and his mother was with us until November. Up and downstairs I ran for potties, hotties etc, and before long we managed to get her down at midday and then eventually she returned to London.

It was a frustrating year as far as the job was concerned, as the abattoir never actually materialised and we found that we simply could not manage on the money. In many other ways, it was wonderful being in England all the time. It enabled Pipyn to go to Launceton College and take her GCE 'O' levels and we were able to have Penny and Nigel and their two sons for a long stay in our very own home. Nigel allowed Poo to come back early so that we had extra time with her and her boys – gorgeous, gorgeous cuddly children! Duncan, the second boy, was born in Ibadan, Nigeria on 11th January 1964 and he really was a poppet. Penny and Nigel had bought a very nice house at Sandsend near Whitby, and we three went up to stay with them over Whitsun and were there for Duncan Rory Limont's christening. Dominic clung to me during the service, chiefly because I had a handbag full of sweets to which he helped himself continuously. He loved his nanna – even if it was only cupboard love!

Our cup of joy was full when Peter arrived back on leave, but in the meantime Ben had signed on the dotted line with the Crown Agents to return to Sierra Leone. He also went up to London for an interview for the job of Director of Protocol, Hong Kong. His name was one of two sent forward for the Hong Kong government to select one man... and the other chap got the job, chiefly because he was fluent French speaking and already in the Foreign Office. We were sad when the Ministry of

Development rang to tell us the news. Perhaps we were even sadder in 1966 when we were told he could have had the job after all, for the other candidate turned the post down. However, by then we had signed our contract and the ministry knew it was no good offering the position to us!

Peter rang one night from Amsterdam (which Pipyn thought was in Canada for a few moments!), for he had come back via Hong Kong, Taiwan, Japan, Honolulu, Canada and Holland; and when we were all together it seemed as if it were only yesterday that he had left us. I think perhaps that is the most wonderfully rewarding thing about our family, that the length of separation makes no difference, as our ties seem to just get even stronger.

Peter was only with us for about three weeks when we set sail for Sierra Leone again, but this time from London in a cargo-passenger ship, the Sulima. First we had to spend a week in London together in a flat lent to us by Air Vice Marshal Sir Edward and Lady Gordon Jones, Margie being Penny's godmother. During this time Pipyn went down to Cambridge to stay with the Spuds who had moved there. It was on the Battle of Britain Sunday, after we had been to a lovely service in St Clement Danes, that we got back to the flat to find Ben had left a tap running in the kitchen and the water had overflowed and dripped through the downstairs ceiling! Five floors up we were, and the whole thing had tremendous possibilities! Poor Ben! He was so upset as you can imagine, but the occupants of the underneath flat were absolutely charming and promised to send us the bill for redecoration if necessary, but never did. The following day Ben took out an insurance policy against ever doing anything like that again.

There was a strike on at London docks and our departure kept being delayed. We went down to spend three days with Dottie and Orby Wise at Westgate-on-Sea which was very pleasant, and eventually sailed on 30th September 1964. There were twelve passengers of whom three were nuns who proved to be the greatest fun and the biggest Bingo fans of us all. There was another girl Pipyn's age on board, and she and Pipyn had the greatest fun. It was a non-stop run to Freetown, arriving on the 10th October and anchoring offshore until the morning where we were met by Finch Field and the Jarrats', but Finch gave us the good news that we were posted up-country to Sefadu, Kono District on a special duties task in the Diamond Protected Area.

The voyage had been remarkably successful, for it had had such a bad beginning: just as we were about to cast off the purser came into the cabin to see if all was well; we said it was, apart from the fact that we had no cabin or 'Wanted On Board' luggage! After much consternation, it was eventually discovered that all our kit had been stowed in the forward hatch underneath five thousand bags of cement! Pipyn and I each had a couple of summer dresses that had arrived too late at the cottage to be included in the heavy loads, but poor Ben had nothing tropical to wear apart from a suit he had bought at the last moment. He had to borrow shorts etc from the captain. We all managed somehow, but it was with much relief that we caught sight of our things after we had been in Freetown for a couple of days. Even then there was still one crate missing as the things were being put on to the lorry. Again after much searching, it was discovered in some remote corner of the ship! Many apologies all round and 'all's well that ends well'.

After four days in the government rest house in Freetown we flew up to Yengama, about three hundred miles away. Just as we were about to board the aircraft Ben was handed a telegram saying, "Proceed to Kenema, not Yengama." The Kenema plane was full, but the pilot of the Yengama aircraft said he would drop his other passengers and fly back to Kenema for us. However, when we arrived at the mine airfield at Yengama, he put his head around the door and said, "Those passengers wishing to proceed to Kenema can not now do so, for I have to return direct to Freetown as the other aircraft has had an emergency and this one is needed by the Prime Minister."

So there we were, stranded in the middle of Africa: no hotels; rest houses; or any visible means of support!.. or so we thought. Luckily Ben had 'fussed' a little at Hastings and had insisted on not being separated from our luggage and had had it taken off the other plane so that it could accompany us – how wise he proved to be!

We walked over to the little hangar feeling very dejected, to speak to a small cluster of Europeans gathered there. There was a woman amongst them and when we looked at each other she said, "I am sure we have met somewhere before," to which I replied, "Yes, I am certain we have. My name is Boult." "Mine is Nutt!" she answered. There was much laughter from the spectators, but sure enough we had met in 1951 when her husband was one of the instructors on Ben's RAF station at Wellesbourne. Anyway, from then on we were wonderfully looked after and accommodated in the mine rest house, a lovely little bungalow with super tiled floors and air conditioning. We called on the District Officer at Sefadu that afternoon, and I can still see the look of horror when he heard of our arrival! The house we were to live in was still occupied by an American Peace Corps chap and we very obviously weren't wanted. However, he was very nice when we explained what had happened.

After about four days we were able to move into our permanent home in Sefadu, about ten miles from Yengama. It too was a very nice bungalow, no air conditioning or fans of course, only spasmodic electric light, and from time to time no water – but we were wonderfully happy. Two other European couples were living nearby and, once we had got the grass cleared from the front door (it was nine inches high!), we had quite a nice view and eventually I made a nice garden. Our loads arrived too, taking four days and three lorries to make the trip, for it was in the middle of the rains and the roads were just a sea of mud in places. There was one patch on the road where the mud was about two feet deep and a Land Rover was standing by permanently to tow cars and lorries through, for a sum of course! No pay, no tow, it was as simple as that.

We had a very good steward called Brimah; a garden boy who was a treasure called Temba; and a night watchman who slept well! Temba and I got on very well together and he soon cottoned on to the fact that I preferred zinnias to cassava. His English was very bad and we had some rather ghastly mistakes. One of the funniest of these was when I asked him to find me a woman from the village to help with the washing. "Woman?" he said. "Me no understand." "You, man. Me, woman," I told him. "Oh yes, oh yes I savvez," he grinned and the following morning turned up with a boy saying, "Here missus, your wash-woman!"

Although the house was painted and scrubbed from top to bottom, we never cured the cockroaches. We also had two very nasty black crab spiders on different occasions and one night, a huge scorpion appeared on the ceiling of the veranda. However, the watchman happened to be awake and dispensed with it for us! Another evening too, we heard a palaver in the hen house and Ben and the watchman went to investigate. There was a cobra, black with a red throat and a mouth full of baby chick. Ben killed it and brought it up on to the veranda for me to see – a horrible sight.

Another morning Brimah was late with the early tea and when we went to see why, rather irritably we found him and the watchman battling with millions upon millions of ants which had invaded the kitchen and were making there way into the dining room. It was a most ghastly sight and took us hours to clean up after we had 'flitted' and put paraffin down. The ants were in everything, inside the stove even. We had two more visitations from ants, but neither as bad as this. On the last occasion the ants marched past the house for four hours in columns of hundreds. The hissing noise they made was fantastic to listen to, and the 'human' bridges they made from time to time were fascinating. These migrations only seem to happen at the end of the rains, and the Africans say that it is a sign that there are no snakes about, but in our case that was not true.

Sierra Leone up-country where we were was very hilly and much drier than near the coast. During the 'winter months' of December to March, the Harmattan blows from the Sahara Desert and the countryside can become covered with dust and the atmosphere very hazy. The nights are chilly too and it is cold enough to wear a cardigan in the early mornings. Flying over what seemed endless jungle to get to Kono District was fun too. Occasionally one would see a little clearing containing a hut or two with no visible outlet to the outside world. How often my thoughts strayed back, not too many years really, to the days when people walked through that frightful bush with its mosquitoes and snakes. I often wondered too as to how the soldiers had any energy left for fighting the enemy after having had to battle with nature first. There is a stone monument in the jungle-bush near Kainkordu to the British and French soldiers who fought each other in 1893 when they each thought they were fighting a certain dissident tribe. The tribe crept out from between them, and left the two European armies (or companies) facing each other and many casualties were caused before the situation was realised.

Peter was to spend a month with us from the beginning of November, and he enjoyed himself although he was a little shattered at the bushness of our life after Penny's lovely house in Kaduna. It was wonderful having him to stay and the days simply flew. He went on one or two treks with Alan Salter of the mines department, and he and Pipyn went down to Kenema for the weekend and brought back a lovely alsatian puppy with them, to be called Carlos. Peter and I used to try to shop in Koidu. I say 'try' as one could hardly ever get what was necessary as there were usually no potatoes etc, but of course one could get everything for a Mercedes! Koidu is an incredible place and I suppose millions of pounds have been made there, by Africans and Lebanese alike, underneath those hot tin roofs. However, the town boasted no sewerage, street lighting or laid on water; and the hospital had no laboratory, refrigeration or X-ray!

Money, money, money and the evil of diamonds, for one could see very little good coming from those precious stones. The people's minds had become twisted and corrupt and the terrible thing was that one didn't know who to trust as there was bribery in everything. I suppose the biggest compliment that Ben could ever have been paid was that he was never offered any inducements, although one chap used to bring pounds and pounds of liver to the house 'for missus' (which Carlos enjoyed) – but this particular chap was refused a permit, so it didn't get him very far! We were given some lovely presents when we left though: an ivory mask and a beautiful leopard skin being among them.

Pipyn found plenty to occupy her time and worked for her Spanish and Latin 'O' levels which she passed, and took a bookkeeping diploma, which she obtained. She also taught herself shorthand and typing and was much to be admired in her perseverance which she inherited from her father! I learnt to cut hair and make bread. I know that these are poor attributes, but perhaps better than nothing! It all began because someone in Koidu wanted one pound to cut Ben's hair, which worked out at about a penny a strand!

Ben's job was extremely difficult and frustrating. He was Secretary and Chairman, more often than not, of the Residential Permit Board which consisted of himself, the Chief of Police Officer, and the Paramount Chief of the district or their representatives. Although they had twenty-two thousand applicants and interviewed some fourteen thousand before we left, the disheartening thing was that so often known illicit miners, with police records, who had previously been turned down for permits were before long in possession of the necessary document to allow them to reside in Kono. Someone's pocket in Freetown must have been lined as that particular piece of paper could cost anything up to £1,500.

In July Ben, Pipyn and I went on a month's trek to a place called Jaiama Sewafe, even deeper into the bush. Nothing was there in the rest house, apart from a bath – but we loved it all! It was here that I learnt not to have even the slightest belief in my stars, for the local paper, which was sent out to us, said something about 'exciting telephone calls' and as we hadn't had a telephone for over a year, it shook my 'faith' somewhat! We took everything we could think of to Jaiama of course, apart from food, beds, nets etc. We had the sewing machine, and last but not least, piled on top of everything in the back of the old Land Rover, old Pa Cook. We also had Carlos with us, who gave us the protection that the sleeping policeman on the back veranda never could do.

Near Jaiama there is a place called Massabendu where people were dying like flies daily from disease and many were also killed by falls of sand as they were digging for diamonds illicitly. The army was sent in at one stage, after two rival tribes had fought over illicit diggings and had complained to the prime minister that the other was encroaching on ground where no one was supposed to be anyway! Nothing much ever came of it, apart from the fact that several soldiers returned to base somewhat the richer for their exploits.

In December 1965 Pipyn had to return home as the government would not pay her fare after she was eighteen. We two were left on our own for the very first time for twenty-seven years! It seemed a bad beginning to our loneliness when I tripped and fell into a drain while carrying the afternoon tea tray and broke my ankle, although we didn't know that for a month and thought it was only torn ligaments. Ben rushed to my aid and sprained his ankle too! Anyway, it meant Christmas was spent in bed and we were tied to the house for three months, for we had no transport as our car had been shipped to Freetown on the back of a lorry to be sold and the Land Rover had 'died' on us. All the same, it was a happy time and we built many castles in the air and had lots of poppers-in, mostly during the afternoons when we would be having tea in the garden, or 'in the street' as Brimah used to call it. I got very attached to Brimah.

New Year's Eve brought a distressing letter from Teddy, Ben's brother in Zambia. He had got himself into debt and we had to mortgage our gratuity and cancel our Morris 1100 car which we had ordered ready to meet us at Liverpool. However, out of the blue came a letter from Miss Daw in the Ministry of Defence asking if Ben would be interested in going to the Turks and Caicos Islands. Yes, of course... but where were they?!

From then on we built many castles in the air and had plenty of time to do so, for we had no transport and of course, I couldn't walk. Lots of people came to see us, and the Africans in particular were so kind and friendly while our fellow Europeans, our nearest neighbours, were so unthoughtful and extraordinary. Several people spring to mind such as the sister in charge of Koidu Hospital, who used to pop in often to see how I was and who brought me endless pieces of tailors' cuttings for my patchwork. She was a Jamaican and her husband was a charming African. Also there was our neighbour on the other side, the man in charge of the electricity, whose name was Bright – straight out of happy families. We used to call him Power Bright and his great friend was Sam Foster, now a judge, who came from the Gambia and who used to come and see us whenever he was in Kono District. One night he took us to see the Guinea Ballet. This was a really excellent, exciting performance and very slick. Although everything was in their local dialect, we could understand what was going on, for the miming was so good. Two little boy drummers almost stole the show though.

Brimah, our steward, was very good on the whole and we had developed quite an affection for him. He was particularly moved when I came back from hospital with my leg 'in concrete' as he called it and when the time came for us to leave we tried hard to fix him up with a job, but it was all very difficult. We left Sefadu on the 9th March 1966 sadly, for we had made many friends. The office had collected a purse for us, half of which we gave to the Koidu Hospital and another ten pounds to a blind albino. It was a kind thought though, and we appreciated it very much.

Kono... so many things I haven't mentioned! It was the district where people develop a stoop from walking with their heads bent down looking for diamonds, and so often finding them. Many a fortune has been made and many lost, and many lives too. We used to hear of several unhappy events, among them the arrest of a European who was later sentenced to imprisonment after waiting a year for trial. Since then his appeal has been allowed, and he has now left the country. Amusing stories too, one of how the bank manager was awoken one night, or rather before the crack of dawn, by a Lebanese who said he was sorry to disturb him but he had bought a diamond for £20,000 and hadn't *quite* enough cash in the house! Mercedes cars were used as part payment for stones in many cases, with the price of the diamonds being low and a car thrown in for good measure. It was quite amazing the type of people who owned Mercedes' – the prison keeper for example!

Life was very expensive in Kono. Nobody bothered to grow anything, for they were all far too busy panning, mostly illicitly, and fruit etc was only obtainable at a high price. The largest sum I think I can recall was nine shillings for a small cabbage, a lot of money in 1965! Needless to say, I didn't pay and we had the usual tinned peas instead.

Before Pipyn left she gave Carlos to the Chief of Police who we spent our last two nights with him and his nice wife. Unfortunately I was feeling very sick, so wasn't particularly jolly and was unable to go to a curry lunch which the Parkers and the mine manager gave for us. However, on the Monday I somehow made the aircraft – and it was so full, and so hot! There were three stops on the way, and we were not allowed out until eventually we reached Hastings, and Lynn McCartney was there to meet us. I shall never forget the absolute heaven of her air-conditioned bedroom, straight to bed I went and stayed there until the following morning. Then lunch, but I was still feeling awful and it was thought that I had had dengue fever. Poor Ben was terribly busy, trying to get his money (gratuity) out of the government, as it would have been fatal to leave without it. He also had to have a medical, X-ray etc, and eventually on Friday afternoon he was in the clear with the cheque in the bank to pay off the overdraft we had on Teddy's behalf. We moved to the Dorman's for a couple of days and they very kindly sent us to the boat early on Saturday morning and we were on board before anyone else. They came to see us off later with two bottles of champagne.

It was a lovely restful trip until about three days out of Liverpool when we ran into a force ten gale. I had to retire to my bunk. I wasn't actually sick, but just petrified! The Salters, who had been in Sefadu with us for a while, were in the opposite cabin and they both succumbed. It was most demoralising to hear the stewardesses nattering outside the cabins with such encouraging remarks as, "Gusts of ninety miles per hour I hear," followed by the crash of a tray! The sea was a sight, a great terrible sight, with waves forty feet high and washing over the sun deck. Ben was loving it of course! Lifelines were everywhere and I'll never forget how the Andrews liver salts chased the vegetable laxative up and down the shelf one evening until Ben returned from dinner and wedged them down! We were twelve hours late arriving and when we did eventually step ashore, it was snowing!

Mildred Hinchley came to see us, I haven't told you about her. It was the most pathetic moment of our tour when one evening we were sitting on the veranda in Sefadu and an African came dashing in and said, "Come quick, the PWD master sick bad. I think too late." We leapt into the car and, sure enough when we got to their house, poor George was dead and Mildred beside herself. He had been to see us that morning and had said he was feeling tired. Apparently, when he became ill Mildred had sent for the local MO who arrived to find her giving him the kiss of life and was so moved by the sight that he turned away, burst into tears and left her. I took her home while Ben and Myrtle Vandi, the nice sister from the hospital I have mentioned in Koidu, arranged things and had the body taken down to Freetown that night for burial two days later. Mildred then flew down to the coast accompanied by Natt Vandi and eventually flew home in a Britannia. We had packed up all her belongings for her and sent them off by sea, but she later told us that when they arrived, her things were all soaking and mouldy and had obviously been left out in the rain. Also, she was *still* waiting for some money from the government ten months after George's death. She was very brave, and it was so good of her to come and see us when we arrived in England.

~ Chapter Eight ~

THE CARIBBEAN

We spent the rest of the night in Liverpool and then drove down to London in our Mini Traveller, arriving at about 5.00pm to have tea with Granny and Pipyn. It was wonderful to see them both again and the next day we did a little shopping at Barkers and took Miss Daw to lunch. Afterwards, Ben had to go for an interview and then we still had to wait for confirmation of the appointment in writing, although he was told that he had the job. With three months leave in front of us, somehow we had so much to do. We found the cottage in an awful state, no carpet down etc, but we buckled too and it was lovely to be home again. Soon it was time for Ben to go up to London to fetch his mother who was very surprised and pleased with the new room we had had built on. After she left, Bess, Val and many other poppers-in came, and the time simply flew. All the while, we were trying to get the house painted and complete the packing for our next adventure. I was feeling rotten most of the time too, for some unknown reason – and it was so maddening.

There was great excitement when Penny and her three arrived at the end of May. Three gorgeous, if somewhat noisy and determined, children and we love them all dearly. Dominic is the intellect, Duncan the comic and Dariel too young at the moment to define, but she will be like Dominic I think. We handed over the top of the house to them and Pipyn retired to the new room!

In the middle of June I went on a course with Ben, to the Overseas Service College which was held in Farnham Castle, Sussex. We went up on the Sunday and on the Monday I had one of the worst headaches I can remember having. However, by Tuesday I was able to go down with him to the castle, although I didn't go to the briefing. It was a lovely place and we had the most enjoyable week learning a lot about other people's places, but not much about the Caicos Islands! For the first three days they couldn't even find a map, but then someone came down to give us a private interview, but he had only been on a two day visit to the islands! It was all great fun though and we eventually travelled out with one of our fellow 'students', Bob Besant, who was going to the Cayman Islands with his wife and family to be CPO.

We left London Airport on the 29th June 1966, by VC10 (Super) for New York, and to my amazement, we actually left on time! We were driven out to the airport by Ernest Whiteside-Jones and the whole thing went so smoothly, apart from the ten minutes when Ben was flying! Not true! I am always given the most wonderful strength to go through things, and I think I have at last learnt to rely with all my heart on the Almighty. Myself the week before, and myself during the journey were two different people. How can I ever show enough gratitude for so many blessings?

New York was covered in smog and we didn't see a thing. It was hot and sticky too and our treatment, like criminals, was most discouraging and I don't think I ever want to go there again for pleasure. We spent a couple of hours at the airport locked in a lounge, and then took off for Nassau. We arrived there in the pouring rain at about 7.30pm and it was just as dark, hot and sticky as New York, but we were soon through customs and were very pleasantly surprised to find a Government House car waiting for us and a very nice driver who apologised for the fact that Sir Foley or Lady Newns were unable to meet us. We enjoyed the drive into town, so lush and green and somehow as one imagines the Bahamas, but of course we couldn't see much as it was so dark. A great welcome awaited us at the Newns', and we were so thankful to go to bed fairly early. At least it was early for them but dreadfully late for us, for by UK time it was about 3.30am as there are seven hours difference. We were to discover later that it took us about two weeks to get over the time change. How people flit hither and thither, I can't imagine!

The next day Ben had to go to the office for a little and we were both bidden to lunch at Government House, which was a very pleasant affair in a lovely old colonial building with Sir Ralph and Lady Grey being charming hosts. Afterwards we were taken for a little drive and then had tea with the Bamforths, whom we had known in Sierra Leone and who had asked Alec Murray over too. Alec had been the agricultural officer in Freetown when we last saw him. It was a very nice afternoon together, then that evening we went to a dinner party given by the Newns, and then thankfully to bed, but not for too long as we had to be at the airport at 7.30am for the last leg of the journey to the Turks Islands. It was a three hour journey in an old Dakota where I think we were the only European passengers; it was like something out of a film. The others on board were loaded to the hilt with packages and brown paper parcels, and we were soon to know why: shopping in the islands was virtually nil! One could have been in Africa too, for of course they were almost all of African decent. Most of the female passengers had extremely large rears and the narrow passage down the middle of the aircraft was a great source of difficulty. One dear old soul in front of us was huddled into her seat clutching her Bible furiously, which she was reading with great zest so as not to notice the flying. I have every sympathy for her as I too have to try so hard to think of something to take my mind off the unnaturalness of it all. This time I contented myself as best I could with looking down at the sea which was the most unbelievable colours, from white to deep blue with all the shades of green in between. After about one and three quarters of an hour we reached Inagua, where we all had to bundle out and wait around in the mosquito ridden heat while customs and immigration checked the aircraft and its occupants. We also had to pay seven shillings and six pence a head for some reason or another because we were leaving the Bahamas and going on to a colony. The Turks and Caicos Islands were one of the last remaining British Colonies and were what was known as a 'grant in aid colony' and received more financial help in relation to their population than anywhere else. All the same, they were very poor and only just managed to struggle along with that help and the help of Oxfam, for the rains had failed for the past five years and there were no crops.

Thankfully we climbed back into the DC 3 and landed at South Caicos about an hour later. The sea around the island was almost transparent and it was possible to see shells on the ocean bed as one came into land, for the end of the runway was not many yards from the shore. The airfield was unpaved as the Americans say, and consisted of a surface of crushed coral. All that has changed now, for when we left two years later McAlpines were hard at work laying tarmac, 'MacOil-Pines' as the locals called them. Anyway here we were at last, but we had to go to Grand Turk for the weekend as the guests of the Administrator, and then return to Cockburn Harbour the following Monday to take up residence. On the airstrip there were a number of people to meet us including: Bert Malcolm, who was the government officer and was to be Ben's number one; the fisheries officer; and a lady doctor. Both the latter were Europeans, while Bert was a Caicos Islander and a most awfully nice chap.

I stayed in the plane but the others came in to see me and I was rather put off when I said to Pat, the doctor, that I was glad she was on the island as at least there would be another female for me to talk to, for there wasn't another wife out there. She replied to the effect that she wouldn't have time to see much of me! I was to learn later that she was a very difficult person and terribly within herself, although I got to like her very much on the whole. Tim the fisheries officer was an odd character. He was very pushy and tried to take precedence over Bert; the atmosphere was far from happy.

At Grand Turk there was a large airfield made by the Americans for the use of their two bases in the islands, which were given to them in exchange for destroyers during the last war. We were met by the Goldings, who were very nice and so friendly. On to Government House, this was a nice old building and we had the guest rooms with their own balcony overlooking lovely white sands and blue seas. By this time it was lunch and after that a nap and a swim. I could hardly believe we had really arrived. We had brought the Goldings out a stilton cheese by request and were delighted to be relieved of it, for it was beginning to be rather high – no one on the Bahama Airlines flight had anything on us! We had a cocktail party that night; and the next day went on a sightseeing tour and a trip around the island with Terence Ford in his very ancient Land Rover. He was a most amusing and charming chap who was the assistant administrator. There were more parties on Saturday night, in fact a dinner given by Terence; and then on Sunday a lunch time session at Government House where we met endless people, both locals and ex-pats.

Monday came at last and we went over to Caicos on the BAL flight at midday and to the one and only hotel, The Admiral's Arms, a sort of transit rest house for pilots flying in from the USA and around the Caribbean, where we were to spend a week before moving into our house. It was July, very hot and the hotel had no fans or air-conditioning and I did feel it rather. The manager, Liam McGuire, was very helpful and his charming wife Lynn, so kind. We in fact spent only about four days at the hotel and with their help, and the loan of lots of things, moved up into our large, old wooden house which looked exactly like the ark after it had been stranded on Mount Ararat. Ben started working immediately of course, and luckily I had my tapestry as there was nothing else to do and nowhere to go, but I was happy to sit on the veranda in the lovely breeze, for being high up we got a lot of air. Sometimes we got too much air, and it took us several nights to get used to the continual hard flapping of the curtains. This sound reminded us of the noise that must have occurred on the ships in the olden days, when their canvas was buffeted by the wind. We were not the only occupants of the house, lots of rats and cockroaches, but somehow one had got used to them in other parts of the world and while they were never pleasant, they are bearable if one doesn't let them get one down!

The house was high on the only hill at Cockburn Harbour and was virtually built on rock. It had large concrete catchments around it to catch every little drop of rain and drain it into a nearby tank. It was from this tank we got the water for the house, being hand pumped into another tank above the house twice a day. There was no hot water at all and when I wanted a bath I had to boil kettles – Ben was content with cold showers. The bathroom and loo were downstairs and midnight sorties were a nuisance, for the stairs were very steep and long.

Of course I wanted to start gardening and I could see only one solution: to garden in tubs. So I sent one of the old men, who were on government relief and whose job it was to help me in the garden, in search of any old oil drums that he could find. Everyone thought I was crazy, but in no time I had about a dozen drums all sawn off at the same height, painted red and planted up against the veranda. They were slowly filled by another old man who had a donkey cart. He went around the island grubbing up soil from nooks and crannies, for there was no depth of soil anywhere. Eventually, I got the tubs planted with zinnias, marigolds and some other gay flowers, but plant selection was a process of elimination, for a lot of things would not grow because of the length of day and the amount of salt in the air, which was terrific. Everything rotted from the salty atmosphere including curtains, cottons etc, and everything that was rustable, rusted. Tomatoes, cucumbers and melons did well, and they were all watered with the waste water from the kitchen and bathroom. In no time at all we were eating a few home grown things and my patch of lawn, about nine foot by nine foot, was the wonder of all, and the only lawn in Caicos!

The house was on top of a hill and we had the approach road mended and the hillside cleared, this seemed to show up the Union Jack, which we very proudly flew near our gate. At the bottom of our 'garden' was the lighthouse, a very feeble thing which we said was lit by two candle power. However, because of this lighthouse, we had a generator which also worked the lights for the doctor's house, the DC's office and the dispensary. The lights were very poor and did not allow one to sew at nights, but at least it was better than oil lamps.

About the second day we were there Ben went to Providenciales with Liam leaving at about 4.30am to catch the tide and getting back as the sun set, at about 6.30pm. He said he enjoyed his day and that the sea was quite unbelievable, as for miles and miles it was no deeper than four feet. At one place though, off the west coast, there was a completely circular piece of deep, deep blue water known as the round hole. Its existence seemed to have no definite explanation, although it was believed to have been made by a meteorite. As you can imagine, with local superstitions running rife, the place was considered fathomless and full of beasties and hobgoblins!

Ben had his own official outboard boat, the Sea Cat, and he was to make many a trip in this. It was fun for him, but I am such a coward about the sea that I am ashamed to say I never accompanied him. Often he would leave before dawn and do a visit to some outlying settlement. He would visit places where, if it had been fortunate enough to have rain about ten days previously, mosquitoes would be out in full force. These mosquitoes were worse than can be imagined, a man's shirt would literally be black with them and in one place, Lorrimers, even the donkeys had to be covered with sacking to prevent them dying from bites. One can only wonder why anyone should choose to live there. They are not an anopheles type of mosquito, but extremely unpleasant and do give a sort of fever. An expert once came from the Cayman Islands to see what could be done with this problem, but he said it would cost a fantastic amount as the area was so vast. Apparently these mosquitoes breed in the sand and scrub, can lie dormant for up to six months, and then hatch out after the slightest little bit of moisture.

When there was no wind we got sand flies too, but we would often look at the view from our veranda, which was simply beautiful, and think what hundreds of pounds people would pay to come and look at it! The town was very untidy and spread in all directions and the endless donkeys, cows and uncontrolled dogs were a great menace. There were wild horses too, the descendants of those animals which used to pull the carriages in the heydays of Caicos, when there was a sisal plantation and apparently lots of trees which brought the rain, and a big salt industry. The latter had to close because of economics, but of course the salt pans remained, the roads were made of salt which at full moon was a gorgeous sight – like a warm frost!

There was nothing much to do apart from go to The Admiral's Arms for a drink occasionally or to have a meal, but that was expensive. Instead, at night we would often go fishing off the end of the little pier and, although we were not very lucky, it could be exciting when Ben landed a shark. Sometimes we would see myriads of floating lights, a thing we have never come across before, which were caused by creatures which looked like seaborne glow-worms. The locals said they were a kind of worm or jelly fish, but not phosphorescent!

Talking of fishing, I was keen but extremely inexpert and unlucky, although I did catch a huge fish once by myself! However, one Sunday afternoon I managed to get the hook, after a magnificent(?) cast, into the ball of my middle finger of my right hand. There was at the time no doctor on Caicos, but we dug the nurse out and she had about four goes at trying to extract the hook. With no anaesthetic of any sort she wasn't getting far, so we decided to ask Lew Whinnery, an American pilot who was flying from island to island with a new set up, who said he had removed hooks before. Ben went to fetch him and returned with Whinnery who had come with a pair of pliers. He nipped off the end ring, gave it a twist and pulled the hook through, which was painful as you can imagine. Afterwards we all three went back to The Admiral's Arms for a drink, as the men said they were so shaken that they had to have something! The nurse gave me some penicillin and it was amazing how quickly the hole healed, but it did put me off fishing for some considerable time.

At a certain time of the year we used to get a lot of hermit crabs and one night in our back yard, we counted one hundred and forty-seven of them and then gave up. It was amazing the noise they made with their shells on the rocky base of the yard and, until we discovered what it was, we were quite mystified. There were no snakes on the islands and I only saw one scorpion. There were not many birds either, but we did have some lovely humming birds and I used to put cotton wool out for them which they would pick at and fly off to use for their nests. I often tried very hard to find a nest, but never did.

At the end of the island there was a LORAN station run and owned by the Americans, and was somewhere that we went occasionally and where Pipyn went frequently – she being the only young girl on the islands! She had a wonderful time really and was sorry to leave. She got a job working for Liam and also managed to get a flight to Florida, through his firm, and a free trip to Jamaica where she spent three days. Later, when

Peter came out and Valerie was also with us, the three of them went to Haiti for a long weekend.

Pipyn once got a lift on a British destroyer to Turks Island! We awoke one morning to see the ship lying off, and there was great excitement as no one knew she was coming or what nationality she belonged to. With Cuba being much in the news and not all that far away, we thought perhaps we were being invaded. However, we soon saw the ensign and, in due course, four officers came to lunch. There was panic on my part for a time as there was no shopping as I have already said, hence visitors always presented a problem, although they were more than welcome. Frantic notes had to be sent to the hotel, who produced the inevitable chicken – we provided the inevitable tinned peas! However, it was all great fun and very refreshing and Pipyn was offered a lift over on to HMS Leopard. She told us afterwards of how she had had her leg pulled unmercifully and how she had been told that they had been diverted etc and she would have to go to Antigua with them. Apparently it was all so well done that she almost believed them. It was a great experience for her and they gave her a ship's crest, which she added to her collection of souvenirs, amongst which is a sailor's cap from HMS Britannia, which we picked up near Lumley Beach in Sierra Leone.

We had only been on the island about six weeks when there was a hurricane warning. These days warnings are given well in advance and in fact one tracks them for at least a week before they are anywhere near one's habitation. In the olden days however, it was a very different matter. The lack of birds, the movement of the ocean and the complete quietness apparently were the best warnings. Even then of course, no one knew when they would be hit. We heard lots of tales of hurricane 'Donna' in 1935 which did a tremendous amount of damage and cost the lives of about forty fishermen who were out lobster catching and were caught completely unaware. One of the people who went through that hurricane said that it was the most beautiful moonlight night and, as he walked home from a party, he wouldn't have believed it possible that within an hour and a half the town would have been hit and all the main roads flooded. Tidal waves do perhaps the most damage, but although one usually imagines these waves to be a complete wall of water like the Severn Bore, they are not. They are created by the gradual massing of water to a great depth which just has to go somewhere, and have an appearance like a slow moving wall.

However, back to our hurricane called 'Inez'. As the forecasts got gloomier and gloomier as far as Caicos was concerned, we put up the shutters and battened down. The Administrator spoke to everyone over the local radio, which was provided by Cable and Wireless. In fact he gave a five minute bulletin every day at 1.30pm, and it was all most touching when he ended by saying, "God bless and guard you all." Lynn and I were sitting on the sofa in our house when we heard him. It really was moving and quite horrid waiting for something dreadful to happen. We looked down on the town, so still and rather dusty for there were the occasional small whirlwinds. The plan was that we would evacuate our house as it was considered unsafe in high winds and it would not be possible for anyone to get up the hill to us if they needed any help that we could give. So we packed a bag, took the dog and moved into the hotel where the other ex-pats had gathered too. 'Inez' sat off the island about ninety miles away all night, and then decided to move off in another unpredictable direction. However, we did have a terrific storm where the rain beat down and we couldn't hear ourselves speak. It was hot in the hotel too, for Liam had put up the zinc storm shutters. We all made fun of it, and in some ways when nothing frantic happened it was a sort of anti-climax, although of course we realised how extremely lucky we had been. We went back to the house the following day, but in a few weeks time we were battening down again, just in case. But once again, thank goodness, all went well and no damage was done, but on this occasion Cuba followed by the Gulf of Mexico suffered dreadfully.

1967 passed away very quickly with lots of visitors, mostly Americans who were staging through the islands en route to San Juan or some other such places. We made a lot of very kind friends who always brought us some luxury, which was a great thrill. Luxury is not perhaps as one would normally consider such a thing to be but chocolates, fruit and even soft margarine were unobtainable most of the time, and these as gifts meant so much. Above all – plants! In no time at all I had a hedge of different coloured bougainvillaea growing in tubs and cascading over the wall. We had no real hurricane scare that year thank goodness, although there were some possibilities which didn't materialise. Ben was very busy and did a lot of touring which was usually very hard work and meant a lot of walking. During such walks he would outpace the locals on the straight but they would catch up with him on the inclines. It was fun to see him striding out and as one of the islanders said, "I love to see the Captain walk." He gained much admiration for his military stride!

We were asked over to Grand Turk for Christmas 1967 to spend it with our new administrator, Robin Wainwright, whom we had met in Singapore when he was on a visit with the IDC. He and his wife were tremendous value, even though she did rather rule him with a rod of iron. We had a very pleasant time although Ben did have a gippy tummy for the 25th, but he was able to enjoy lunch in a careful sort of way. Lunch was followed by a rest and then a lovely swim. We thought of our many friends shivering at home and, as we had had a lovely shower of rain, everything had a brand new look to it. So often we used to see the rain out to sea and it was so awful to witness all that fresh water going to waste when we were so desperate. At one time we were rationed to one gallon of fresh water per person per day – only that in a hot climate!

In January 1968 Grandma Steer came to stay for six weeks. She was a very good guest, no trouble at all, but it must have been very dull for her, for of course there was literally nothing to do and nowhere to go. Just before Grandma Steer left, Val arrived, whom it was lovely to see. However, Val was in a great state of nerves and tenseness and was very often tearful. She took over the job of nurse in Caicos while a new one was being sought, and her first call was early one morning when someone arrived to say that a child had drunk kerosene. However, Val coped.

We had at this time a super lady doctor standing in for a few weeks, Elizabeth Johnson, and she is one of the people I most admire in this world. Her sister had died of cancer, she had had a breast operation, she had another sickly sister and a very old frail mother; so hence she could only manage a short locum. Even with all this, she never grumbled and was a really dedicated person, trekking miles to see her patients. She was so different from her relief who was only 'here for the sunshine and to make some money' and didn't appear to have a calling at all. However Val, I think, enjoyed her time with us and it certainly did her good, for we sent her home very fit.

Val stayed on an extra week so that she could see Peter, who was spending six weeks with us out of his long leave, having been to England and Canada en route. He and his girl friend, Susan Denton, bought me a super pair of white sandals in Montreal – shoes being another impossible thing to buy in Caicos. Shopping did improve as time went on, but everything was desperately expensive. Even so, when we left at the end of

July 1968 there was no chemist or baker's shop. It was terrific having Peter, who with Pipyn went on several swimming and diving expeditions and brought back some super shells. He was with us for our thirtieth wedding anniversary where we all went out to dinner at The Admiral's Arms and he made a touching speech.

Pipyn was getting restless, she felt that she wasn't really doing enough and of course, things were very limited. She had her horse, Nimrod, which was more out of the stable than in and we spent endless hours catching him. The 'we' is rather a poetic license as she did most of the catching with the aid of several local lads. We had also acquired a lovely alsatian bitch, Bella, from the States, but feeding her properly was quite impossible and eventually we gave her to a couple who were posted to the Bahamas.

Peter left in April and in May we had the first South Caicos Regatta which Ben started and organised and which was said by all to be a great success. The Governor of the Bahamas and Lady Grey came down and the day was fine, with the wind blowing and a great time was had by all. The sloops from Providenciales began the day by arriving at the end of their race, which had started the afternoon before the big day. It was a lovely sight to see them in full sail. There were all sorts of different races and, as none of the islanders had ever taken part in a regatta before, the races were begun from an anchored start as no one had any idea of crossing a starting line!

Soon after the regatta Jan arrived to stay until it was time for us to go on leave. She was in a state of 'nerves' and badly needed the rest and change, but we shall never know what had upset her. It seemed obviously something that had happened in Jordan before she left there, where she had been OC Nursing Service, Jordan Arab Army. I suppose too that I was 'down', as the saying goes, and she somehow played on my tenseness and kept pointing out the disgusting state of affairs (as far as she was concerned – although we no longer looked at it like that!) of having to put up with cockroaches, rats and mice, not to mention the gnats and mosquitoes at times. Anyway, somehow or other she sowed the seed of discontentment in my mind. I think if I had known that basically I was suffering from hypothyroid and agoraphobia, I would have had a different outlook on things, knowing that there was a cure and that these things could be coped with. Anyway, be that as it may, we decided secretly, I think, that we would not return to the islands. To this day it is one of those decisions I wish with all my heart we had not made.

The days went by rapidly and we packed in between swimming and Jan going off on various boating expeditions with Ben and Pipyn in the Sea Cat. On one occasion when the boat got stuck going to Lorrimers, Ben and the boatman, Fon, jumped out to push; and Jan's eyes apparently almost popped-out of her head, for they had been out of sight of land yet the water was only about two feet deep.

Eventually the day came for us to leave, and it dawned with threatening clouds and hopes of rain, it was July 1968. As we sat at breakfast that morning on the veranda I remember so well seeing a flight of gorgeous flamingos go overhead in a patch of blue sky and my heart was heavy. Fritz Luddington, who had his own plane, offered us a lift to Nassau and for which we were grateful because we thought it would be so much nicer than flying there in the old Dakota of Bahama Airlines, but when we were airborne (Fritz, the pilot, Embury, Ben, Pipyn, Jan and myself) he announced that he wanted to 'pop in' at Providenciales for lunch to see how things were progressing at the Third Turtle. My heart sank because all I wanted to do was *get* to Nassau! However, I coped – had to, I suppose! We were met at Provo by a Jeep and were driven to lunch at the hotel, and continued afterwards, getting to Nassau just ahead of several aeroplanes that were stacking up to land. Fritz made a sharp turn and we were in, my tummy having been up to my throat and down again.

We stayed at the Washington Hotel, for we had two days before boarding the Canberra, and it was all rather fun really and we so enjoyed the food, fat as I was. Yes really fat, and I didn't realise how much so until I saw myself in a long mirror, for we hadn't had such a thing on Caicos and every time I needed clothes, they were made just that little bit larger! Anyway Nassau was great, and we had rides in the horse driven buggies and went to the Aquarium. This was most fascinating as there was a huge round glass tank holding all the various fish that could be found in the Caribbean, and where twice a day a diver would descend to feed them by hand, be they barracuda, shark or turtle! There was also a very clever performing dolphin which caused great amusement.

Another day we went to see the drilling flamingos – quite a show. As one goes in, the old boy in charge would present anyone wearing shorts or a mini skirt with an apron to cover up the 'indecency' and then, after a slight lecture on morals etc, the birds were produced and they did drill according to his instructions: 'left', 'right', 'halt' etc. It was a lovely sight to see these graceful pink birds doing what they were told. I wrote to Johnny Morris about them and I often wonder if he ever went to see them. The other nice thing about Nassau in my mind was the basket market and, of course, I had to buy one, although Pipyn said I didn't really need it. It is still with us and most useful.

    The day dawned for us to board the Canberra and we had a very nice outside two berth cabin, although Jan and Pipyn were not so lucky and poor Jan lived in fear of the Goanese crew somehow. The journey was quite uneventful and the weather unbelievable, with the sea so calm that, as Ben said, one could have rowed across the Atlantic. We didn't stop anywhere, but just glimpsed Bermuda one morning. At least we didn't stop until we got to Cherbourg where it was raining and foggy so we didn't go ashore, as we were to land at Southampton the following morning. It was here we had a Morris 1100 Traveller awaiting us, in white. This was a very nice car, although those two girls in the back seat couldn't see out very easily. We had so much luggage that a lot of it had to be put on the roof, which caused the wind to make a whistling noise and the polythene covering to flap; this noise caused Jan much distress! We went up to London and as always after one has been away sometime, were struck by the neatness of the little gardens and the masses of roses everywhere. We stayed in Kensington at a nice hotel and Jan took Pipyn out on a shopping expedition the following morning after our arrival. Meanwhile, Ben and I retired to the Standard Bank of South Africa to try to sort out Aunt Vi's will, as she had died in Rhodesia, and her estate was all most complicated. It was while we were there, I had a dreadful dizzy attack and Ben had to take me back to the hotel where I lay down while he went to Lloyds Bank to see Mr Hogg.

    After a couple of days in London we went down to Eastbourne to see Bess and Val and stayed in a hotel near the station. They were just the same, Bess terribly crippled and Val terribly overworked but so patient and much to be admired. Val appeared to be very strung-up and living on drugs and my heart did go out to her. How she coped with night duty and the chores during the day I shall never know, but they got on very well and I think had much in common.

    From Eastbourne we wended our way down to the cottage – I remember in pouring rain! It was wonderful fun to be going back to the wee house and also to see the pale blue Aga which we had had installed while we were in the West Indies – it lived up to expectation! The cottage was as sweet and home-like as ever and we wondered how on earth we had ever left it. We also persuaded Ben that the sitting room would look super if the modern brick fireplace was taken out and the original inglenook fireplace exposed. He reluctantly agreed to the alteration, for both he and the builder had their doubts about the wall holding together. When the operation did take place, we all waited with baited breath while a labourer placed the new beam in position to replace the ancient one which was rotten. Lo and behold everything held and the room *did* look wonderful and much bigger once the dust had subsided. Ben then painted it black inside, and with the white walls and an imitation log fire it was the perfect alteration. It had a small baker's oven recess too, and we so often tried to picture what had been cooked there about three hundred and fifty years previously.

~ Chapter Nine ~

HOME?

All this time we were trying to pluck up courage to write to Robin Wainwright explaining that I was ill (no one had then decided what was the matter with me) and that we would not be returning to Caicos. There was also the problem of what job Ben would get, but things resolved themselves when we went up to London and met some friends of Jan's, who said that the Royal Corinthian Yacht Club at Burnham-on-Crouch was looking for a new secretary. Ben applied and got the position and we found ourselves going down to Essex to have a look! It was such a flat county after glorious Devon. Then there was the problem of where were we to live, but we eventually found someone who was willing to let us their flat, for a vast amount of money. We took it as we were determined to be together, but decided that when we got there, we would look for something else. Anyway, we moved in October 1968 and it was a lovely flat, right on the river, and the job seemed to be ideal at first.

Pipyn was now attending the London School of Languages learning French, Spanish and shorthand too. She worked hard and did very well attaining her objective of joining P&O on 29th October 1969, becoming a woman assistant purser. When she had finished at the school, she did one year at head office before getting her first ship on 3rd August 1970. At first she did standby duties on the Arcadia, but eventually went to sea on the Oriana. When at last the day came for her to sail, she only just managed it, or rather the ship did, for by the time they had got to the Isle of Wight smoke was pouring from the ship's engine room and so it had to return to port, where they were delayed for several days. No one knew that Pipyn had such a dynamic personality! She loved her life at sea and we were to collect her several times from the ship, for shore leaves. She has been through the Panama Canal at least fourteen times. Eventually she was transferred to the Spirit of London on 17th February 1973, which sailed out of Los Angeles, for Acapulco to Alaska. She flew to Los Angeles in a jumbo jet and enjoyed it and said it was the only way to fly. She lost her heart while on this ship to John Le Cornu, although we didn't know much about it. Eventually she did come back to England in 1974 and John retired from the service later. They became engaged and were married in February 1975 in Crofton Church, Starcross, Devon – but all that comes later; I digress!

While in the flat we did find somewhere else, a small detached house in Brickwall Close, which we bought and moved into during the frost and snow of January 1969. Our loads came up from Devon and the cottage was put on the market. We spent a lot of money on this house, but when another one came up for sale opposite the Club with a magnificent view, we decided to buy it. We sold our Brickwall Close house well and easily. Our new house, 1 The Belvedere, was semi-detached, modern and lovely, but Ben was not happy in his work and well do I remember how one day, when we were both in bed with flu, he sat up and said, "I'm retiring!"

Plans, more plans, and we decided to go back to the cottage, which had not yet sold. Again we did this in the winter of early 1970 staying one night en route at the 'Croft'. I remember how I had written to Aunt Flo saying not to bother about a *big* meal, but little did I expect that we would be offered a boiled egg, "If you like to get it yourself!" We had hoped for something a little more substantial having only had a snack on the journey. Anyway, early the next morning we went to Hayne Barton and job hunting began once more. This time it was to prove more difficult, but Ben did become a recorder for the Milk Marketing Board, getting up early to get to the farms for the early morning milking etc, and coming home covered in muck donated by not too grateful cows. He gave this job up after finding out it was costing *us* money for him to go to work as we had to pay our own stamps etc.

He then applied for the job of a second rate clerk in Launceston, but was told he hadn't the required qualifications! All this, after being to Staff Colleges etc, and having been an administrative officer in the Civil Service and in the District Commission. After a long wrangling, he got an apology from London saying that they had checked on his qualifications and he was eligible for a job of such standard – all this because he had said at the beginning, to the eighteen year old that interviewed him, that he had School Certificate and not GCE papers! Anyway, things took a wonderful turn when he applied for and got the job of organiser for the British Heart Foundation of Devon and Cornwall, raising money for research. He was able to work from the cottage of course, and we bought a caravan eventually as an office. It was a rewarding job, even if it did mean long hours, late nights and much travelling.

During all this time, things had been happening family wise, as the Americans would say. Peter had become engaged to a very sweet Chinese girl, who had been educated at Roedean and spoke less Chinese than he did. His engagement was broken off however in the summer of 1970 and, to help him get over his sadness, he and Pipyn went on a 'grand tour' of the Continent in a Rover car that he had bought from Nigel. On that trip they visited many countries, among them Switzerland, France, Germany and Italy. They went to see the Churches (Rev and Mrs!) in Florence, who had been our neighbours in Changi and were then living in Italy as George was an archdeacon and in charge of the English community in Florence. They also bought me a lovely marble bird bath from a famous quarry.

After Peter had returned to Devon he took us up to Scotland at his expense to see our grandson Dominic, who was a boarder at St Mary's School in Melrose. It was a lovely trip and Dominic, I think, enjoyed his day out, especially his time at the local fair where he won a goldfish! Peter in due course went back to Malaya, but not before he had taken Pipyn and her room mate out to dinner and a show in London. That evening was to have wonderful consequences; for having met Nicky, Pipyn's pal, he never forgot her and in fact fell in love all over again, but this time even more so if that were possible. Later he was to meet her in Singapore as she was also with P&O, and still later again Peter proposed to her when in Holland, much to everyone's joy, for they were so admirably suited. Peter and Nicky were eventually married from his house, in which we were then living, at Dawlish Warren in January 1973. Nicky's parents and some friends came over for the wedding and Bill Kneel, a friend of Uncle John's who had a Rolls, offered to take her to the church and then to the reception, but he *almost* lost the way to the house and Nicky was almost late at the church. Bill was a super chap: big and jolly; and as you can gather, a little direction vague. It was a lovely wedding in spite of the weather being bitter, it was almost snowing while the photographs were being taken. The couple later had a honeymoon in Switzerland before returning to Malaya.

Poor Penny was in hospital, having had an operation to her bladder and I was broken hearted when I rang her up to tell her all about the wedding. However, she was in tears because she was in such pain, but rang back later and was overjoyed to hear details of everything.

In 1968 Nigel had been posted to Cambodia and it was from there that Penny flew home to put Dominic to school. Again she was absolutely distraught when she rang us from Melrose the evening she had first left him in the hands of matron. We tried to tell her that the parents always feel it more than the children, but how helpless one feels at the end of a telephone when one can't physically touch the hurt person. All this happened while we were at 1 The Belvedere, and it was here that Nigel came home to, before going up to Yorkshire and their holiday house. It was here too that we left them with their three for a couple of days while we went up to London for one of Ben's yacht club meetings. However, when we arrived back earlier than expected, we found a man with a huge window pane making his way to our gate. We weren't supposed to have known that the boys had broken the glass while playing cricket! We spent Christmas 1969, with them in Sandsend near Whitby, and all went to church that morning in the dark, with Dariel insisting on wearing a cowboy suit, paper chinese topped hat and sunglasses.

Dominic used to fly out to Cambodia for his holidays and Penny was teaching Duncan in Phnom Penh. It was from here that she brought the three children home in 1971. It was en route in Bangkok that Duncan walked through a glass door and had a four hour operation on his right foot. The operation was a marvellous job and he now has complete use of his foot with hardly a scar to show for the episode. But poor Penny! She was of course delayed, and the Thais were very particular about that sort of thing. If one overstayed one's permitted time, there was usually a fine of a thousand pounds, but in this case they were generous to her. She arrived at Heathrow with Duncan in plaster and Dariel with a very high temperature and during the flight the aircraft captain had radioed ahead for an ambulance. Peter had come up from Hayne Barton, having got a two day extension to his leave, and Dariel was put into Uxbridge Hospital with measles and pneumonia. Peter brought the boys down to the cottage and we looked after them for about a week before the two girls arrived.

Later that year Duncan went to school with Dominic and in January 1971 Penny, Nigel and family (the boys being in Phnom Penh for their holidays) were all evacuated home after a frightful experience. Things were really hotting up in Cambodia at that time, and it was with joy that we welcomed them off the aircraft at Heathrow, although they were (the adults) both in rather a state and much relieved to be safe and sound.

The company (BAT) was good to Nigel and posted him to their head office in London, so they bought a house at Bookham, Surrey from where he commuted up to town every day. It was a super house and they did some alterations and additions. We had many a happy time there with them, motoring up from Devon, but it was in a way an unfulfilling life for Nigel, who one day decided that he could no longer bear the thought of commuting for years and decided to chuck it all in and go 'self sufficient'. This was a very plucky thing to do when his future with BAT looked so assured. We were all full of admiration for them and were so happy when we heard that he had bought a moorland farm near Whitby, where his parents lived.

It was not a big farm by some standards, but more than enough for them to cope with. And cope they did in the most wonderful manner, making the final move up in December 1975. Nigel went up first, then Penny and the loads followed a few weeks later. The house at Leith Rigg needed a great deal done to it and this they set about doing by altering the kitchen first and installing an oil fired Aga. Nigel bought sheep and Dun Galloways together with the usual hens, pigs, geese, ducks, dogs, a house cow called Gertie and two goats – and Penny didn't even like dogs! However, she took to her new life full of her usual zest and before long was up to the elbows(!) in everything, literally, and even helped Nigel with the delivering of calves and lambs.

Nigel, as always, was so methodical, hard working and a wonderful organiser. The two of them made a super pair of farm labourers! They coped with the bad weather wonderfully and really worked almost every hour that God gave them, making a go of things. Then Penny opened a beauty salon in Whitby and worked there for five days during the week, milking early in the morning and late in the evenings. Both of them grew fitter and fitter and looked, and were, so happy. The goats went, a pony arrived and things began to take shape in lots of ways. Nigel bought the neighbouring farm with its house and so had more land and flocks to look after. They also had an extra house on their hands which they did up and furnished themselves, and then let it to holiday makers. We had such happy times with them and in some ways were able to help a little, but had one abortive sortie in February 1978 when we came up from Devon to let them go on holiday. It snowed so hard that we were all snowed in for a few days and they were only able to go off for a day at a time.

However, later in the year they went to Jersey for a week and Ben and I managed to hold the fort without anything ghastly happening.

Back a bit! In 1971 when Pipyn was still with P&O, Ben and I went on an 'assisted' cruise on the Iberia, meaning of course that we got a reduction in fares. We had a super cabin, the most wonderful weather and the North Sea was like a mill pond as we wended our way to Bergen. We loved that city and went up the rack and pinion railway to the hills above to get a full view of the lovely bay. Another day we went on a bus tour to another fjord and also to visit Grieg's house in the woods. The open market in Bergen was full of lovely flowers and our cruise up the Stavanger Fjord was something I shall always remember: bright sunlight; and snow capped mountains, so close to the ship that one felt one could almost lean out and touch them. Then we returned back to Copenhagen. This was another lovely city, but the strip shows etc were very much in evidence by the pictures in shop windows and the chaps on the pavements soliciting visitors. We went on a bus tour too and saw the castle in which Shakespeare set his play Hamlet – an impressive building. Then off around the countryside which was nice but very flat. The city lights at night were fun, and it was with some sorrow that we left and sailed for home, for we had had a lovely time: nice companions; super weather; and good food, although some people grumbled as some always will. While we were away cruising Polly, our corgi, gave birth to five lovely little puppies and she and her husband, Mr Pimm, were very proud and good parents. The dogs had gone to a friend, Maureen Payne, while we were away and she coped with the arrival of their offspring.

All this time we were still in our lovely Devon thatched cottage, Hayne Barton. We used to see the three old ones as we called them, my aunt and two uncles from Starcross, fairly regularly and it was obvious that before very long something would have to be done about caring for them. It was this thought that sadly decided us in 1972 to move, but more of that later. I was still unwell and we went to a homeopathic doctor in Exeter, Dr Kilsby, and he certainly helped me a lot, even though it was only in losing about two stone! It was quite a bother extracting vegetable juices etc, but it was worthwhile.

One evening when we were driving into Exeter to meet Anneke, a dutch friend of Pipyn's who was coming down for the weekend, I had the most awful attack of dizziness etc. After resting in a hotel room and feeling really ill, Ben borrowed a mattress and took me back to the cottage with them in the back of the Mini. Poor Anneke! Ben had to ring the station master in Exeter to ask him to explain to her that we were unable to meet her and would she get a taxi to the Bay Tree Motel. She was very hesitant to do this of course, as she wasn't sure that the request was genuine and wondered what she was in for! However, when Ben's name was mentioned she was happier, but was overjoyed when she actually saw him, and much relieved. The doctor came to see me the next day, and after various tests and a trip to Plymouth's Freedom Fields Hospital where I took radioactive iodine, it was decided that it was my thyroid that was at fault.

Then came the palaver of selling the cottage, a thing which with hindsight, I wish with all my heart we had not done. We had no bother getting rid of it and sold it to a very nice major and his wife. They were a young couple who did a lot of 'renovating' which we think has spoilt it. However, that is neither here nor there now. Peter had bought a delightful modern bungalow near Starcross called 'Conifers' and we moved into this, with the two corgis, on 12th May 1972. It was a complete change but we loved it and I made a very nice garden. Ben had brought the office caravan with us and, after much manipulating, got it through the gate of a field about a hundred yards from the house. He then connected the electric light himself at the cost of five pounds when the official estimate was thirty-five pounds, but of course he had got the blessing of the electricity board before doing so. Rene, his secretary, moved with us and bought a mobile home about three quarters of a mile away and continued her work for Ben. However, she left us in 1974 and Ben had a succession of secretaries who were all nice, but it was difficult to get anyone permanent as the job was very low paid, as it was all for a charity. Understandably they moved when better things arose.

In 1973 Pipyn was moved from the Oriana to the Spirit of London, a promotion really as this latter ship was a prestige ship that sailed out of Los Angeles and ploughed between Acapulco and Alaska. Pipyn flew out in a jumbo jet to join her ship, but although she left with much hesitation as she did not relish the idea of the flight, she later assured me that it was the only way to go, in a big aircraft. She was so happy to be going, as she was to join up with John Le Cornu with whom she had fallen in love. He was an assistant purser and they had been together on the Oriana. On 22nd June 1973, she came home and they were to become engaged later, but while waiting for him to return from America in August, she joined us on a super trip aboard the Orsova. We had a lovely cabin and she managed to get a berth in a not so good one, but it did cost her practically nothing. In fact she won the amount of her fare the first night at bingo – she couldn't grumble! We went to Tangier which was fun, and awoke desert longings in all of us. Perhaps the most amusing thing there was a sign proclaiming real 'Yorkshire Fish & Chips' in the middle of the kasbah! Then on to Rosas, Marseilles, Ville Franche, Ajaccio, Palma and Barcelona. It was a most memorable trip with perhaps the nastiest part being the return to the ship at Ville Franche. While we had been ashore a great swell had arisen and as the ship was anchored off, in order to embark we had to go through the swell in the lifeboats which swayed and rolled with the currents alarmingly. We all made it apart from the last lifeboat which could not come alongside to be made secure, it had to be towed out to sea a bit before being hoisted aboard. One of the crew had a nasty gashed hand.

After we had been home sometime John arrived back, as did Peter and Nicky on leave. Pipyn and John became engaged and the wedding was set for February 1974. This was a lovely affair with Pipyn wearing a long white dress and cape with a hood trimmed with white fur. Dariel was bridesmaid in gold velvet and we all had a very happy day, until it came to about 10.30pm when Nigel rang from half way up to London to say that he had left his briefcase with important papers on the dining room table. Ben wanted to take it up to Bookham but we said no as he was very tired, and so we managed to hire a taxi which took the case for us. It was imperative that Nigel had the papers as among them was an air ticket, and he was due to leave Heathrow on the Monday for a trip to America. Poor Ben, to this day he is very sad when he thinks about it, and *so* wishes that he had made the effort and insisted on going up to Surrey. When Pipyn and John got to the Carlton Towers for their first night, they were greeted by a hotel official wanting to know where the baby was as Pearl, John's sister, had telephoned earlier for a baby-sitter to be waiting to look after their infant while they had a night on the town! We all thought it was hilariously funny, and so did Pipyn and John, who the next day went to Aviemore in Scotland before returning to Jersey where they were to live.

In the January before they were married, Ben and I went to Jersey to meet John's parents and stayed in Pipyn's delightful little flat. I am never keen on flying at the best of times, but as the day of our departure dawned it was dull, wet and blowing a gale. Everyone informed me that it would be all right, so we took-off and the aircraft dropped out of the sky and rose again, only to bump up and down all the way to Jersey. It fell so noticeably that Peter rang to know if we had arrived unharmed! On arrival on the tarmac at Jersey we couldn't stand still, as the force of the wind was so great. We loved Jersey and also John's parents, and our three days flew too quickly. The return flight was uneventful and I felt that I had accomplished something. I think I don't really hate flying, just talk myself into being afraid; and live by the maxim that if God meant us to fly he wouldn't have invented the railways.

All this time Ben was working for the British Heart Foundation and had many drives to the furthermost ends of Cornwall and all stops between for his fund raising activities and committee meetings. Some of the drives were in lovely sunny weather, on spring days and on frosty mornings; but a lot of them too were done at night when it was pouring, sleeting, snowing or even in fog. All the same, he was 'happy in his work' and did a wonderful job. We also had several holidays in Wales where we had found a lovely little hotel near Dolgellau and from which we fished on the atomic research reservoir at Trawsfynydd. Here we caught quite a number of trout and, on one occasion, a super salmon in the river water that belonged to the hotel – this happened on our last day! We went up to Yorkshire several times and always loved our trips, especially the happy Christmases we had with Penny and her family. We particularly enjoyed the Christmas of 1977, when we were joined by Pipyn and John; and the Christmas of 1978, when Wendy and Donald and their three joined us all.

In 1974 my brother Marshall came over from Rhodesia – I had not seen him since 1943! It was a lovely reunion as we picked up just where we had left off and were all very happy together. He was of course much entertained by the Croft inmates, as Uncle John used to refer to themselves, in more ways than one; for he found them all most odd characters. Not least of all Aunt Flo, who beckoned him to go over to the sofa where she was sitting and, with great secrecy, gave him a tiny parcel whispering, "Don't mention this to your Uncle," who happened to be out at the time. We could hardly wait to get to the car to see what she had bestowed on Marshall, and great was our mirth when we discovered that it was a fifty pence! And he a 'boy' of sixty! I suppose when one is ninety, sixty seems quite young enough to still want pocket money to buy ice cream! That summer when Marshall came, we had a drought and he couldn't believe that it usually rained every summer in England, for the same thing happened when he came again two years later. During his stay he spent some of his time carrying buckets of bath water to my precious plants. He was about the most contented person I have ever met, never a grumble or a swear word. Yet he was almost blind and had had a very sad life, his wife having died a few years ago of a heart attack, and he always relied on her to be his eyesight.

We also had one gorgeous trip to Scotland going right up to Cape Wrath on the western side and returned down the east coast. We had perfect weather, and in October we could sit on the side of a loch on the northernmost tip of Scotland, having our picnic lunch in shirt sleeves, watching the seals play in the water and hearing deer in the mountains.

In 1975 we had the wonderful news that Nicky had given birth to a son in Malaysia, called Adrian, and it was with wonderful joy that we greeted them at Exeter Station towards the end of the year. He was the most beautiful baby. In 1977 he was joined by his equally beautiful sister Margriet, so Nicky and Peter had a perfect family, and we now had five grandchildren.

That same year I had an operation, a hysterectomy, and spent two luxurious weeks in the Nuffield Hospital in Exeter. I was very spoilt, but it was wonderful to have got it over and to return to Ben's loving care and a great welcome from our two corgis. The operation didn't worry me physically, but mentally I was very low and bitchy! I was tearful too and hard to live with, but everyone showed endless patience, especially when I took to my bed with my head causing problems. I felt as if I was continuously swaying or on board a ship, with everything dripping and lurching when I was lying still in my bed. This lasted for three months and was the worst part of it all.

During that time Uncle John died. It was very sad because the day before he had had a heart attack he had asked Ben to arrange a health visitor to come in the mornings and give them all breakfast. Auntie Flo didn't approve of this organisation and told Ben to, "Bring your uncle to me," while she still sat in her usual glorious state of oblivion as to what was really going on. Ben replied that Uncle John could do no such thing as he had had a heart attack and was really ill, to which she replied, "It will do him no harm." Ben then said something to the effect that if she wasn't careful he would be found dead in the morning. And of course he was, by the health visitor as she opened the door for the first time. We were all terribly upset. He was such a dear old man and I can see him now coming to visit me when I came out of hospital, in a force nine gale, carrying a bottle of honey upside down so that everything was sticky, but he was a poppet.

Aunt Flo didn't seem at all upset and continued her sessions on her sofa in a land of imagination and incontinence! She would tell everyone how she had been for a walk 'that morning' to pick raspberries, when she hadn't in fact even moved, not even to the loo. Poor old dear, it was all so sad, and she was to be the last to die as Uncle Rufus had gangrene in both feet and refused treatment until it was too late. Eventually he died in Dawlish Hospital where Aunt Flo was at the time for a rest. In fact she was there to give me a rest, as I was over at the Croft everyday cooking etc. We dreaded telling her of Rufus's death, but all she said was, "Fancy him doing a thing like that to me," which showed her current mental state. She remained on at the Croft getting smellier and smellier and more and more difficult. We moved in to live there at her request, but after a fortnight or so she just said, "Get out!" So we did, and eventually got her into an old peoples' home in Dawlish where she was cleaned up and properly looked after. She always wanted to go back to the Croft, which was so sad as it was to be sold and everything in it.

Just after I had my operation Bob Bradley came to stay for two weeks, but his visit dragged on for three months. In the mental state that I was in plus the physical weakness, his stay wasn't a great success, although I hope he didn't realise it. He and Ben had been chums since 216 Squadron days in Egypt in 1933 and it was now 1975. In this year too we had a visit from my American cousin Julia Lewis, who flew over for just a week. We met her at Heathrow and all had such fun. She spent a lot of time at the Croft and was an emotional person and was most upset when it came to farewells. Pipyn came over too in November to look after me for a week and did a wonderful job of spring cleaning the bathroom, which I hadn't touched! Teddy was staying with us at this time too, before Bob arrived. Anyway, one way and another it wasn't a quiet convalescence!

~ Chapter Ten ~

A FINAL NOTE

Well I think that is all, or almost all, for I shall add some odd events that have sprung to mind since writing these pages.

I think you all know most of our movements since we moved to Yorkshire on 21st March 1978, three or four years earlier than we had intended. Penny came down to see us in Devon and found me not well and us having too many visitors. So she said to Ben, "Daddy this has to stop. You must retire and come up to Yorkshire." "Yes, darling," he said thinking we would do so in three or four years time. She came back to Whitby and three weeks later rang to say, "Daddy you have bought a flat." So here we are. I hated it for a long time. I missed my garden and found it so difficult pouring a quart into a pint pot but now, at almost seventy-seven, I am grateful not to have so much to do.

Our years have been happy. We got to know our grandchildren here. Peter and Nicky have brought their children up several times, also Pipyn and John come over from Jersey once a year with their gorgeous brood. We have been to visit them in Jersey several times and on one occasion, came back on the ferry on the day of the infamous Fastnet race. Their son J-P, as we call him, plans to go into the RAF. We so hope he does, and that we may live to see him in uniform.

And now to complete our happiness we have a gorgeous great granddaughter, Sophie, given to us by Duncan and Harriet.

We also had a memorable visit to Dartmouth to see Dominic's Passing Out parade, and later to the Royal Naval Air Station at Culdrose where he got his Observer Wings. Sadly for us, he has decided not to make the navy his career.

We also had a lovely trip to Bulawayo and the Victoria Falls in 1980. We went out in answer to an SOS from my brother, Marshall. It so happened we were there for Independence Day and Mr Mugabe made a churchillian speech which we thought boded well for Rhodesia's future, but sadly things are not well in that country now.

The year 1990 began badly with Ben having a stroke and visiting three hospitals for tests and treatment. Wonderfully he was not badly affected, apart from exhaustion and now we no longer go away on visits. We so loved our trips down south and to the Lake District to see Margaret Blackburn, but we are so grateful to be as we are – much more fortunate than most.

Here are a few more things that have stuck in an old lady's mind! On second thoughts, I don't think I'll bother. You've heard it all before a thousand times.

I do want to say that if you are ever in any trouble or distress, remember this marvellous text that Phillip Burkenshaw told us was used by a padre at a service on the eve of the Parachute Regiment going to war:

Fear closed the door
Faith opened it, and
There was nobody there.

~ Appendix 1 ~

A ROUGH RIDE
by Ben Boult

When I woke up on the morning of the 24th July 1944, in my tent on Dunsfold Airfield the sun was shining and the war seemed far away. At briefing, we were told that today's operation would be a maximum effort – the whole wing of three Squadrons in one formation, led by the wing leader, Wing Commander Ling.

The target was a large concentration of German tanks just east of Caen, in Normandy. The met forecast was clear skies over the south of England, but half way over the channel extending south over the whole target area, there was a thick layer of cloud between four and eight thousand feet. Therefore the bombing would be by G-H. This was a method which consisted of two radio beams which were set to intercept at a point in space at twelve thousand feet at which if the bombs were dropped, they would hit the target. Blind bombing, a good idea if it worked! As my Mitchell bomber was one of very few with this device, the wing leader decided to take my aircraft for the operation.

I had recently taken over command of 180 Squadron and had only carried out about ten operations so I decided to fly Number 4 to the wing leader, directly behind him, to see why he was such a successful leader. His ability was recognised by the award of two DSOs (Distinguished Service Order), more than one DFC and similar decorations from France, the Netherlands and Belgium – quite a lad.

Because he was flying my aircraft 180 Squadron would lead the formation, which was a big one. Each Squadron was in a box formation of four flights and each flight was in a box of four aircraft.

The idea was to drop our bombs on the leader's bomb aimer's command, as his was the only aircraft with the special 'box of tricks' to bomb through thick cloud. We were to arrive over the target at twelve thousand feet.

180 SQUADRON

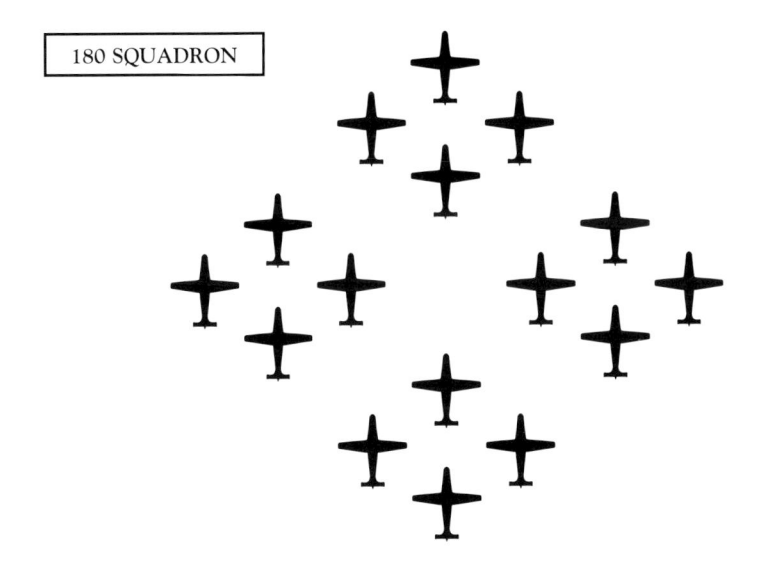

We took-off, joined up and left the south coast at Littlehampton climbing to our operation height of twelve thousand feet – but there was no cloud! Maybe it was a bit further south? No it was not, there was just a slight haze with blue sky overhead.

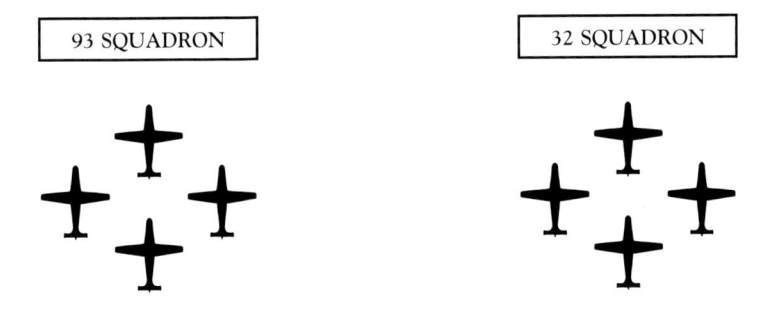

93 SQUADRON

32 SQUADRON

Thus we came to the target which could be seen more or less clearly through the haze, but we were clearly silhouetted against the blue sky and consequently there was plenty of fairly accurate flak.

As we ran into the target, the leader's bomb aimer, who was also a well decorated chap, broadcast the bombing run, "Bombing, bombing, bombing," which should however have been followed finally by, "Go." There followed many interesting curse words as the beams faded out and there was no signal by which to bomb.

Paddy Burgess, my bomb aimer, had followed the run in on his bomb sight as he could see the target through the haze and could have dropped our bombs at the right time, hoping that the rest of the formation would have followed, but that did not happen either as we had probably been hit already by flak which damaged the bomb release.

The whole formation went round again for another run up to the target and at that moment there was a bit of a gap in the proceedings because the next thing I knew I was flying alone – no formation! Looking around I saw the formation about five hundred feet above me with no aircraft Number 4 in the leading flight! I opened the throttle flat out and rejoined the formation and took stock of what had happened as we flew round for the second run.

My second pilot who was a new flight commander, Flight Lieutenant Griffiths, had joined the Squadron the evening before and had just come along for the ride, was now dead with a lump of metal through the heart. One of my two air gunners, Jock, came up to the cockpit and reported the damage: Paddy had collected a piece of shrapnel in his knee, but was OK; and Tich, the other air gunner, had not been wounded. Jock confirmed that the second pilot was dead and so we ran into the target for the second time. I took stock of the 'office': I had a sore head; my right arm was not functioning very well; and most of the instrument panel was in bits with no radio and only two instruments working, my airspeed indicator and the gyro compass. However, both engines and their controls were OK and were the only things I really needed.

On the way round Paddy crawled up to see what was going on in the office and reported that he had been hit in the knee. I told him to go down to his bomb aimer position as we were going round again and off he went for a second dose. He was a brave lad, as he could see the flak coming up from his position in the nose.

As it happened, the second run took us over another formation and the leader stopped his run and said he was going round for a third time which is what we duly did, but sad to say when the command to bomb was given by the leader (now on visual bomb sight) our bombs did not come off. The formation then turned for home and lo and behold, as we turned for home there was the promised blanket of cloud! I realised that in my present state I could not fly in formation without jeopardising the other pilots if we went into cloud, and that even descending through cloud on my own might be tricky. I therefore quickly went down to two thousand feet to get below cloud so as to see where I was going.

I considered landing in the bridgehead but decided to try and get back to England as the engines were performing normally and I was sure that the chaps in the bridgehead would not want us in our state (aircraft and bodies) to add to their problems.

Flying over the Mulberry harbour at less than two thousand feet was a bit dicey as I was sure they were trigger happy poor chaps, but I had no alternative. Having cleared the harbour without incident on our way north, I asked Paddy for a course to set for the nearest UK airfield. He probably was thinking on those terms himself, as he came back almost immediately with a course and ETA for Tangmere. As I set course I felt a bit tired and wondered if I had made the right decision, but there was plenty to think of on the way home to keep me active as in addition to flying the aeroplane, the bombs were still hung up. I was forward thinking to our arrival in the UK!

While Paddy, Jock and Tich were trying to get rid of the bombs, I worked out a plan which might have worked if we could not jettison the bombs. Plan: I would fly eastwards along the south coast; make a dart over an unpopulated area of coast, drop the second pilot out with his parachute on a static line; tell the others to jump and then set my controls for a steady climb over the sea to France; and jump out myself as near to the coast of England as possible. I hoped the aeroplane plus bombs would then crash and blow-up on some vital spot in German occupied France!

While I was wondering if this plan would work, we were thrown up about a hundred feet by an explosion from somewhere underneath and Paddy reported what had happened. All their initial efforts to dislodge the bombs had failed, so he got Jock to hang on to his ankles while he hung head down in the bomb bay to see if he could work the release mechanism. He tried to move the release hook of the nearest bomb by hand and after much effort, the hook sprung open and all the release hooks then sprung open at the same time. There he was with his head almost touching the bombs as they banged together jostling each other, being all primed and activated and ready to explode! However, they gradually bounced their way out of the bomb bay and exploded about five hundred feet below us as they hit the sea, hence the sudden uplift.

To avoid feeling sorry for myself and prevent my mind from wandering after the relief of knowing that the bombs had gone, I concentrated on what we were going to do when we got to Tangmere. The undercarriage was hanging down and the operating lever was useless, the flap lever did not work either and the bomb bay would not shut. However, all this I could cope with and I knew what to do. Paddy knew his stuff and found the correct verey cartridges to indicate we were in trouble and were going to land. Being on the ball, he chose the right signal for the right day as he loaded the pistol and bunged it into the launching chute, all ready.

When we arrived over the airfield I gave the signal to Paddy to fire the pistol and then started my circuit to land. I told the crew to take up crash landing positions and got on with the job in hand.

When flying downwind and across wind I chose the place to touchdown on the grass, to the right of the 'into wind runway'. Then I noticed that there was a Spitfire taxying around the perimeter track towards the runway, coming from right to left and I judged he would be directly under me as I made my final approach. I said bother, or words to that effect, and made an adjustment to my approach which was made a little more difficult as I now had to turn off the fuel in sufficient time to use as much as possible before switching off the ignition, to minimise the risk of fire if things went wrong. As it happened all went well and we missed the Spitfire, and slid along happily on our belly, coming to a stop without further ado.

Jock and Tich got out quickly through the top escape hatch, but Paddy tried the usual hatch in the floor which he had not realised was now hard on the ground. So I pushed him out through the top escape hatch and followed, sliding down over the nose onto the grass.

The 'blood wagon' was there and after a few words, I requested them to ring Dunsfold to tell them where we were and how we were. Paddy and I were then driven away to St Richard's Hospital in Chichester.

ADDENDUM

As you know, my right eye was damaged by bits of flak and I was wounded in the arm and leg. But what you may not know, because there is no visible effect, is that the night I was being cleaned up I asked Paddy, while the doctor was messing me about, to go and look for a silver pencil I thought I left in the blood wagon. People were coming and going, but when he came back, long before I could have seen him I said, "Well, Paddy did you get it?" When the doctor was asked by the specialist if I had any sight in the eye that night he said, "Yes, he recognised his navigator who came into the room on the right side and he could not have seen him with his left eye." The specialist said to the doctor, "If that's the case, I will not take the eye out." In fact I recognised Paddy by his footsteps! It was a game of mine to know people by their footsteps. I used to greet people who came into my office by name without looking up or turning around.

Although I was told not to, I found a mirror three or four days later and had a look at my eye. It was solid red all over – top and bottom and side to side. I could not see a thing for some time. I never knew about the conversation between the surgeon and the doctor at Tangmere until years later – gimmicks can be a good idea!

PS by Peggy Boult

April 1992

It has taken me forty-eight years to hear the above account in detail. Ben was awarded an immediate DFC whilst Paddy received one later too.

As you know, Ben flew again eventually becoming, among other things, the Chief Flying Instructor of the Central Flying School. Also it is interesting to know, that he has fifty-two stitches in his face (some pre-war), and I always tell him it has been a great improvement!

LETTER from Jock & Tich after landing at Tangmere

Dunsfold
25/7/1944

Sir,

Tich and myself are sorry that we didn't see you this afternoon. We got to the hospital just before the operation and naturally the "starched" types wouldn't hear of it. We did see Pat however and he was sitting up in the bed tearing into a plate of soup looking very pleased with life. Life – I guess that we all are eternally indebted to you for keeping us on this earth. Whilst we were with Pat the senior MO from here showed up and offered to take us back with him by road, an offer which we accepted. When we got back here we went over to the intelligence officer to see if he wanted any gen from us. He didn't, but the Group Captain was there and he asked about yourself and Pat. He reckons that you put up a good show, a gross understatement I thought. Skipper, I'm not a flanneler by nature but if I put down here all the things I want to say I'm sure that you would mentally put me into that class. Shall I simply say that you upheld all the traditions of the fighting Irish, and that if you intend to hold them up some more, here is a bloke who would consider it a privilege to be in the same aircraft. Tich says that that goes for him too. All the rest of the Squadron are right behind you and you're a hero skipper. What they think of a certain other pilot is quite the opposite and what they think of him may not meet with your approval but there it is. Tich and myself are people whom nobody, in authority I mean, wants to know but tomorrow we shall see S/Ldr. Fisher and see what's what. If we get some leave we intend to come down and see you and in the meantime we're hoping that you have come through alright. Get well quick skipper, and let's go back and show Jerry that he can't kick us, or should I say you, and get away with it.

Happy Landings!

"Jock & Tich"

~ Appendix 2 ~

GENERATIONS

A CELEBRATION OF AGE – Unknown Author

We are survivors! We were born before penicillin, television, polio jabs, frozen foods, contact lenses, before frisbees and the Pill.

We were born before radar, credit cards, split atoms, laser beams and ball point pens; before tights, spin-driers, electric blankets, dishwashers and air-conditioning. We were born before men walked the moon.

We got married first then lived together afterwards. In our time, having a meaningful relationship meant getting on well with our cousins, while designer jeans were scheming girls.

We thought fast food was what you ate in Lent and outer space was the back seat of the cinema.

We were before gay rights, computer dating and marriages, before dual careers and house-husbands. We were before group therapy, nursing homes and day care centres. We had never heard of FM radio, tape decks, electric typewriters, word processors, heart transplants, yoghurts and guys wearing earrings.

For us, time sharing meant togetherness, not holiday homes or computers. Hardware meant hardware and software wasn't even a word.

In 1944 'Made in Japan' meant junk, and the term 'making out' referred to how you did in an exam. Pizzas, McDonalds, Chinese take-aways and instant coffee were still to come. Goods in Woolworths cost sixpence or less. For tuppence you could take a tram ride, make a phone call, buy a bottle of Tizer or enough stamps to post one letter and two postcards. You could buy a new car for a hundred pounds, but who could afford one? A pity, because petrol was just one shilling a gallon.

In 'our day' cigarette smoking was fashionable, grass was mown, coke was a cold drink, smack was something you got for being naughty and pot was something you cooked in. Rock music was Grandma singing you to sleep and Aids were helpers or assistants.

We were certainly not before the difference between the sexes was discovered, but we were surely before the sex change. We made do with what we had, and we were the last generation that was stupid enough to think you needed a husband to have a baby!

No wonder we were so confused and that there is such a generation gap today.

What better reason for a celebration?

I'M FINE THANK YOU – Unknown Author

There is nothing whatever the matter with me,
I'm as healthy as I can possibly be,
I have arthritis in both of my knees
And when I talk, I talk with a wheeze.
My pulse is weak, and my blood is thin,
But I'm awfully well for the shape that I'm in.

Arch supports I have for my feet,
Or I wouldn't be able to be on the street.
Sleep is denied me night after night,
But every morning I find I'm all right.
My memory's failing, my head's in a spin
But I'm awfully well for the shape that I'm in.

The moral is this, as my tale I unfold
That for you and for me, who are both growing old,
It's better to say, "I'm fine," with a grin,
Than let folks know the real shape we're in.

How do I know that my youth is all spent?
Well, my 'Get up and go' has got up and went.
But I really don't mind when I think with a grin
Of all the grand places my 'get up' has bin.

Old age is golden, I've heard it oft' said,
But sometimes I wonder as I get into bed,
With my ears in the drawer, my teeth in a cup,
My eyes on the table until I wake up.
Ere sleep overtakes me, I say to myself,
"Is there anything else I could lay on the shelf?"

When I was young, my slippers were red,
I could kick up my heels right over my head.
When I was older, my slippers were blue,
But still I could dance the whole night through.
Now I am old, my slippers are black
I walk to the store and I puff my way back.

I get up each morning and dust off my wits
And pick up the paper and read the 'Obits'.
If my name is still missing I know I'm not dead,
So I have a good breakfast and go back to bed!

~ Appendix 3 ~

JOTTINGS

This is really just to amuse myself and most of it you would have heard before but maybe our great grandchildren won't have done so.

I was born on 18th April 1915 in Salisbury, Southern Rhodesia, then a Crown Colony, but now Harare, Zimbabwe. I was christened Margaretta Dorothy Marshall Symons – pronounced 'Simmons'! My father Samuel Marshall Symons had walked up to Bulawayo from Mafeking in 1896 as the railway only reached Rhodesia in 1897. His parents were yeoman farmers in Week St Mary, Cornwall and he was of solid English stock, very kind and patient and never known to swear. He and my mother Dorothy Williams in 1912 were married by the British Consul in Beira, then Portuguese East Africa, now Mozambique. She was born in Cullompton and her father was a vicar, later of Exminster. She was of aristocratic stock, very gentle and kind – and such a big snob! It was an unlikely match but somehow they made a go of it until 1936.

After I was born, my father moved to Umtali, now Mutare, where my brother was born almost blind and was christened Percy Barker Marshall. It was while my parents lived here that my father was shot in the right eye and lost it. He was out shooting game when another party, doing the same, saw the grass move and thought it was a buck. I never heard any more details than that, except that afterwards he had to wear a glass eye. My parents took my brother to Johannesburg and to the Exeter Eye Infirmary to see if anything could be done about his sight. Although a little was achieved, he was never able to go to school and had a tutor after my mother had taught him for some years.

My father was one of two brothers, John and Samuel, and two sisters, Florence and Hilda. My mother had two sisters, Muriel (known as Billy) and Gertie who married a Dr Avery. Auntie Billy went to Rhodesia to help my mother with her children in Umtali and she too, a super person, was very particular. I remember her telling me that she had broken off her engagement to a mounted policeman because he had made slurping noises over his soup! She later married a Mr Gregor in Johannesburg (she was a trained nurse) and when he died she married a James Sims, a provincial commissioner in Basutoland. Going back to my mother, she was a brave soul really and coped with hunting-spiders, snakes and many flies and mosquitoes etc well.

Later my parents moved to Bulawayo where I went to school, and when my father moved to Salisbury my mother remained there. After they were divorced, a big thing in those days, she married Richard Tregarthan Michell and they lived in the Cape Province. I later moved up to Salisbury to be with my father, whom I was very fond of, whilst my brother stayed in Bulawayo. He later married, but had no children. Uncle Dick, as I called my stepfather, had been to the Cambourne School of Mines in Cornwall and was Chief Assayer of the Standard Bank in Bulawayo. He used to show me gold bars and said that if I could lift one I could have it! He and my mother had got together because they were both very horsy minded and did a lot of riding together. In contrast my father was like me, believing that both ends of a horse were dangerous and best given a very wide berth.

Again, going back to my mother, she told me that in Beira they had a huge staff and one boy's sole job was to see that the soda siphons were always full whilst another boy's job was solely to wind the handle of her machine when she wanted to sew. I often laugh at things she used to say and do. One such occasion was the day I said, "Mummy there is an African lady at the door selling eggs. Do you want any?" "My dear," she replied, "there are no African ladies, only African women." Today she would be hung, drawn and quartered for those sort of remarks! The other thing she always used to do was to give any chickens we bought for fattening Epsom salts in their water for the first few days. Her given reason was that, "One never knows where they have been." She would die of shock if she knew that in later years I was to drink water from a mountain stream in Kurdistan, only to find, as I walked further up the hill, that there was an Arab washing in the 'clear' water! It had no ill effects on me.

Aunt Hilda was an entirely different person to Auntie Flo – she was a typical headmistress. Aunt Hilda was cuddly and understanding and I used to love being with her in Taunton in the days before I was married. One day she took me shopping and I bought a super pure wool navy and white hound's tooth coat and skirt for the sum of three pounds and ten shillings (£3.50). At the time I thought I was being extravagant, and with reason, for I had been paid the princely sum of eight pounds a month when I worked in the medical department from which I had to pay my lodging and also dress myself etc. Tennis shoes (trainers) were two shillings and sixpence then and when I came over to England I paid fourteen pounds for my fare from Cape Town to Southampton. I can't recall what the three day train journey down to the Cape cost. In those days Africa was 'safe', we had moonlight picnics out in the bush often, with no fear of being harmed and we never locked doors by day. However, it was considered unwise to leave women alone at night but that was just a precaution. We had the same servants for years.

Uncle John, my father's brother, who was a big pompous, lovable and generous man, joined the army in the First World War as a Private and ended up as a Colonel fighting for the White Russians in 1917/1918. He never married but had been engaged. He was then in the Ordinance Corps which supplied munitions but was called up again in 1940 and served in England.

Uncle John and Auntie Flo had bought a house in Cookwood, 'The Croft', and she lived there while he was away and had two elderly paying guest's, refugees from Switzerland. When I began to be ill I went to stay with her too, taking Peter and Penny with me. It was not a happy time as apart from war worries, she was not a sympathetic person, and I needed sympathy! She was headmistress of the local village school and one day took Penny there for lunch. At that time Penny was only four and apparently, during a silence, said in a loud and clear voice, "Lovely grub." We never discovered where she had heard the word 'grub', but Auntie Flo was very amused. When Aunt Hilda died, her husband Uncle Rufus Ree went to live at 'The Croft'. He often said to me that it was the worst thing that he ever did. He was a very nice man and adored Pipyn, but died of gangrene in 1978 which was very sad. Aunt Flo died that year too, aged ninety-one, whilst Uncle John died the previous year, aged eighty-seven. They were all old and lived off the fat of the land with Devonshire cream every day of their lives – and none the worse for it!

One day when we went to tea, taking with us my brother Marshall who was over from Zimbabwe, Aunt Flo beckoned to him while Uncle John was out of the room and said, "Come here and don't tell your Uncle," handing him a small parcel wrapped in writing paper. We were longing to get outside and see what he had inherited, for I knew Aunt Flo had some gold krugerrands. In the car he unwrapped it – one fifty pence coin! Poor old thing, she was quite simple towards the end. She would tell the hairdresser, who called, that she wouldn't have a shampoo as she didn't like get her hair wet.

It was in 1925 that we, as a family, came over to England. My father was to represent Rhodesia at the Empire Exhibition at Wembley. He returned after a few months, but my mother and we two children stayed on for a year. It was then that Marshall had his eye operations in Exeter whilst we lived in Exmouth. During that time I was a boarder at school for two terms and was terribly homesick.

It was when the ship was approaching Southampton that my father received a wireless message to say that his mother was dying. We went straight to Exmouth and I can just remember being ushered into a bedroom to see a very old lady. In 1937 my father came over again on government business, for the Coronation, and we came over to meet him. My Papa was awarded the OBE then. In about 1930 he played golf with the then Prince of Wales (Duke of Windsor) when he was on a visit to Africa – and my father beat him!

I was presented at Court in 1938 to the Queen Mum (Elizabeth Bowes-Lyon). We were stationed at Kenley at the time and it was all very convenient! I do remember being overawed by it all, the splendour of Buckingham Palace and the beauty of the lovely looking Queen.

I know you have heard of Ben's crash at Mersa Matruh on the 7th July 1936. In brief, he was the captain of the aircraft but had verbal instructions to let the other pilot fly. They were trying to avoid search lights as part of training and were blinded as they were coming into land. Ben realised that they were too low and grabbed the controls, but it was too late. They crashed and burst into flames. Ben managed to crawl a little way away from the wreckage and then was finally dragged to safety by a member of 208 Squadron who accompanied him to hospital in the ambulance. He asked if there was anything he could do for Ben, who asked him, in turn, to send a telegram to Granny saying all was well. The wire was duly sent and received by Nell at the same time as the newspapers had printed headlines about the crash. Six out of eleven occupants of the plane were killed and Ben had his face badly injured. Amongst other things, a huge flap of skin had come away from his chin, which was duly sewn on. He was then allowed to grow a beard, a goatee, as he couldn't shave. He loved it – and I hated it! I was furious when he sent me a photo of him and 'it', to show my friends. 'It' nearly broke the whole thing off. Anyway, eventually he was sewn together, eyelids and all, and best of all perhaps he was exonerated by the Court of Enquiry. With all the various messings about, his face has been greatly improved! I think he is marvellous, but don't tell him! He has fifty-two stitches in all, including war wounds.

ODDS AND ENDS

Silly little things I remember:

The silver bracelet I wear with Peggotty on it was given to me by Ben when he came on leave from Brussels. It had been got for him in Denmark where the price was his cigarette ration and a tin of cocoa – one could buy anything there for cigarettes! It was engraved by a Polish immigrant in Ross-on-Wye.

It was in Ross that one day, as the Italian POWs were being marched by the house, that Peter cried out, "Come and see the Roman soldiers!" Also in Ross, I was out walking one day with Peter, who was then very fair and very white faced, when an American leant out of his tank and said, "Hi ya slug." I was furious.

The piece of granite quartz that is on the floor as a door stopper came from Rhodesia and was given to us by Uncle Dick Michell and it came from the Matopos where Cecil Rhodes is buried. The other stone came from Norway – quite a distance apart!

The little ivory drummer was given to us by a Chief in Kono District, Sierra Leone. Pipyn has the leopard skin that was given to us by Al Haji Mohammed Alfa at Sefadu. The iron pennies on the wall are known as Kissi pennies and were used by that tribe years ago.

On my dressing table the hand mirror belonged to my mother and the hair brushes to Granny Boult.

~ Appendix 4 ~

OBITUARY

GROUP CAPTAIN N. de W. BOULT

Group Captain N. de W. Boult, DFC, AFC, former Chief Instructor, Central Flying School, died on February 5 aged 84. He was born on April 6, 1913.

ONE of the RAF's most outstanding pilots and flying instructors, "Ben" Boult was appointed the first Chief Instructor at the Central Flying School, Little Rissington, in 1947, the top instructor's post in the Service.

He had wide experience of training pilots, both at home and on the African continent. In addition to his Air Force Cross which acknowledged his work on numerous new types of aircraft entering RAF service, he also held the Royal Hellenic Air Force Cross.

Norman de Warrenne Boult was born in Dublin of Anglo-Irish parents. In the West of Ireland he learnt to sail and race dinghies, a passion he indulged at various postings in his service career. At Rossall School he was an outstanding gymnast and diver. When he joined the RAF in 1933 he brought his sharp sense of balance and timing to the art of flying, in which he was assessed as "exceptional". He also qualified as a physical training instructor, and one of his favourite tricks on dining-in nights was to walk along the top of the mess bar on his hands, no matter how much alcohol he had consumed.

His flying training was in Egypt where, in 1936, he survived a crash in which six out of 11 occupants of the aircraft (of which he was not the pilot) were killed. His face, which had been badly damaged, was rebuilt with plastic surgery, but for some time afterwards he had to wear a beard, something not normally allowed in the RAF.

The start of the Second World War saw him at the Central Flying School, then at RAF Upavon, test flying many of the new aircraft then entering service. Like most non-operational pilots he clamoured to be posted to a squadron to see action. However, he was sent instead to Rhodesia as a flying instructor where, later in 1941, he formed and commanded the Rhodesian Central Flying School, for which he was awarded the AFC.

During this period in Africa he was also awarded the Royal Hellenic Air Force Cross for training Greek student pilots. Returning to England in 1944, he was arrested on Paddington station by an alert military policeman who, understandably not recognising the stripes of the RHAFC ribbon, thought that he was an escaped German officer masquerading as an RAF officer with incorrect medal ribbons. Boult was unable to supply the name of his unit since he was then on his way to the Air Ministry to discover his new posting. All was resolved in due course.

Appointed to a Mosquito Pathfinder course, Boult was disappointed to be taken off it to take command of 180 Squadron which flew the Mitchell medium bomber and was at that time in a demoralised state. He rebuilt the squadron and brought it back into action. But he was badly wounded, losing the sight of an eye during an attack on German tank concentrations, north of Caen. For completing the sortie successfully and bringing his severely damaged aircraft back to a belly landing in England, he was awarded an immediate DFC.

After leaving hospital he served on the staff of the Second Tactical Air Force in Belgium and Germany, but subsequently taught himself to fly again, by both day and night, and was, in 1947, appointed Chief Instructor at the Central Flying School. Among subsequent commands was one at RAF Wellesbourne Mountford, Warwickshire, where he was appointed in 1951 to open an advanced flying school during the expansion of the service at the time of the Korean War.

In 1954 he was appointed Senior Air Staff Officer, Iraq Command, which later became Levant Command, and moved to Cyprus. During the Cyprus emergency he had responsibility for supervising the exile of Archbishop Makarios. He later commanded the Fighter Command Air Armament Training School at RAF Acklington, in Northumberland. This was his penultimate appointment; he retired in 1960.

From 1960 to 1968 he was employed through the Crown Agents in Sierra Leone, where he was largely responsible for organising the independence celebrations in 1961, and the Turks and Caicos Islands. After his return to England in 1968 he became regional organiser for the British Heart Foundation in Devon and Cornwall until his final retirement in 1978, after which he and his wife settled in North Yorkshire.

His wife Peggy died in 1996 but he is survived by his son and two daughters.

THE TIMES – 5th March 1998

GROUP CAPTAIN N. de W. BOULT

Group Captain N. de W. Boult, DFC, AFC former Chief Instructor, Central Flying School, died on February 5 aged 84. He was born on April 6, 1913.

ONE of the RAF's most outstanding pilots and flying instructors, "Ben" Boult was appointed the first Chief Instructor at the Central Flying School, Little Rissington, in 1947, the top instructor's post in the Service.

He had wide experience of training pilots, both at home and on the African continent. In addition to his Air Force Cross which acknowledged his work on numerous new types of aircraft entering RAF service, he also held the Royal Hellenic Air Force Cross.

Norman de Warrenne Boult was born in Dublin of Anglo-Irish parents. In the West of Ireland he learnt to sail and race dinghies, a passion he indulged at various postings in his service career. At Rossall School he was an outstanding gymnast and diver. When he joined the RAF in 1933 he brought his sharp sense of balance and timing to the art of flying, in which he was assessed as "exceptional". He also qualified as a physical training instructor, and one of his favourite tricks on dining-in nights was to walk along the top of the mess bar on his hands, no matter how much alcohol he had consumed.

His flying training was in Egypt where, in 1936, he survived a crash in which six out of 11 occupants of the aircraft (of which he was not the pilot) were killed. His face, which had been badly damaged, was rebuilt with plastic surgery, but for some time afterwards he had to wear a beard, something not normally allowed in the RAF.

The start of the Second World War saw him at the Central Flying School, then at RAF Upavon, test flying many of the new aircraft then entering service. Like most non-operational pilots he clamoured to be posted to a squadron to see action. However, he was sent instead to Rhodesia as a flying instructor where, later in 1941, he formed and commanded the Rhodesian Central Flying School, for which he was awarded the AFC.

During this period in Africa he was also awarded the Royal Hellenic Air Force Cross for training Greek student pilots. Returning to England in 1944, he was arrested on Paddington station by an alert military policeman who, understandably not recognising the stripes of the RHAFC ribbon, thought that he was an escaped German officer masquerading as an RAF officer with incorrect medal ribbons. Boult was unable to supply the name of his unit since he was then on his way to the Air Ministry to discover his new posting. All was resolved in due course.

Appointed to a Mosquito Pathfinder course, Boult was disappointed to be taken off it to take command of 180 Squadron which flew the Mitchell medium bomber and was at that time in a demoralised state. He rebuilt the squadron and brought it back into action. But he was badly wounded, losing the sight of an eye during an attack on German tank concentrations, north of Caen. For completing the sortie successfully and bringing his severely damaged aircraft back to a belly landing in England, he was awarded an immediate DFC.

After leaving hospital he served on the staff of the Second Tactical Air Force in Belgium and Germany, but subsequently taught himself to fly again, by both day and night, and was, in 1947, appointed Chief Instructor at the Central Flying School. Among subsequent commands was one at RAF Wellesbourne Mountford, Warwickshire, where he was appointed in 1951 to open an advanced flying school during the expansion of the service at the time of the Korean War.

In 1954 he was appointed Senior Air Staff Officer, Iraq Command, which later became Levant Command, and moved to Cyprus. During the Cyprus emergency he had responsibility of supervising the exile of Archbishop Makarios. He later commanded the Fighter Command Air Armament Training School at RAF Acklington, in Northumberland. This was his penultimate appointment; he retired in 1960.

From 1960 to 1968 he was employed through the Crown Agents: in Sierra Leone, where he was largely responsible for organising the independence celebrations in 1961; and the Turks and Caicos Islands. After returning to England in 1968 he became regional organiser for the British Heart Foundation in Devon and Cornwall until his final retirement in 1978, after which he and his wife settled in North Yorkshire.

His wife Peggy died in 1996 but he is survived by his son and two daughters.

~ Epilogue ~

Margaretta 'Peggy' Dorothy Marshall Boult (née Symons): Born 18th April 1915 Salisbury, Rhodesia; died 11th August 1996, Scarborough hospital, North Yorkshire.

Norman 'Ben' de Warenne Boult: Born 6th April 1913, Dublin; died 5th February 1998, Whitby, North Yorkshire.

Both were cremated and their ashes are buried in the 'wild garden' at Wragby Farm where Pipyn and her family now live, having bought the farm from her sister's family.

Peter Boult (son) married Nicky Eernink on 19th January 1973 in St Mary's Church, Crofton, Dawlish, Devon. They live in Devon and have two children: Adrian Pieter de Warenne Boult (born 10th July 1975) married Rebecca Allgood on the 28th August 2004; and Margriet Nicolette de Warenne Boult (born 25th February 1977).

Penny Brown (daughter) married Nigel Brown in Freetown, Sierra Leone on 16th October 1960 and live in Cancon, Lot et Garonne, France. They have two sons and one daughter:

Dominic Roy de Warenne Brown (born 9th March 1962), married Susan Barry Wallis in Warblington Church, Warblington 8th August 1992 and live in York. They have two children: Hannah Elizabeth Brown (born 26th January 1997) and Phoebe Isabella Brown (born 14th March 2000).

Duncan Rory Limont Brown (born 11th January 1964), married Harriet Claire Stanton Kirk in St George's Church, Bromley on 14th July 1990 and live in Beckenham, Kent. They have three children: Sophie Elizabeth Brown (born 27th April 1991), Laura Kate Brown (born 22nd June 1994) and Charlotte Madeline Olivia Brown (born 12th June 2001).

Dariel Pitt (16th January 1966), married Richard 'Dick' Pitt in St Margaret's Church, Aislaby, North Yorkshire on 7th August 1993 and live in Harrogate, North Yorkshire. They have three children: Cameron Alexander Pitt (born 20th December 1994), Rory Marshall Pitt (born 18th December 1996, and Fraser William Pitt (born 24th July 2000).

ISBN 0-9549697-0-7
Published by Duncan Brown
Produced by RKM Communications, London

Pipyn 'Pip' Le Cornu (daughter) married John Le Cornu and live at Wragby Farm, Fylingdales, North Yorkshire. They have three children: John Philip Marshall Le Cornu (born 12th February 1979), Hazel Penelope Jan Le Cornu (born 10th November 1983) and Sorrelle Dorothy Pipyn Le Cornu (born 10th November 1983).

John Holderness, Peggy's first boyfriend and life long friend, lived in Borrowdale, Harare, Zimbabwe. The last contact was a letter written to Penny on hearing of Ben's death in 1998.